TO AVI AND NOA,

WHO KEEP ME MODERN BUT IN A VERY DIFFERENT WAY.

REAL.

ACKNOWLEDGMENTS

This book represents not just my voice, but the collective wisdom of countless conversations, partnerships, and moments of growth that have shaped my understanding of what truly makes exceptional leadership possible.

First, my deepest gratitude to the remarkable **thought**partners™ at The Grossman Group. The delicate balance you strike between strategic insight and a Heart First approach to serving our clients continually inspires me. You embody the very principles this book explores—leading with empathy, humanity, and authenticity—and I am humbled to work alongside each of you every day. Thank you, Kate, Meg, Kyle, Linda, Jen, K., Chad, Kayla, Lana, Morgan, Mike, Steven, Carolyn, Barbara, the team at Amplify Publishing Group, and countless other partners along the way who have made this book possible.

I'm incredibly grateful to our stellar research partners, Rob Jekielek and Katie Setty, at The Harris Poll. Your rigorous methodology and commitment to understanding the evolving landscape of leadership have provided the ultimate foundation upon which many of the insights in this book stand. Your data and analysis have been instrumental in validating what we've observed in practice—that exceptional leaders lead with their heart, and integrate emotional intelligence with strategic thinking.

To the modern leaders who generously shared their stories and wisdom throughout these pages: Your vulnerability, insights, and real-world experiences bring these leadership principles to life in ways my words alone never could. Your willingness to share both successes and struggles offers readers the gift of learning through your journeys. I'm grateful to:

Aaron Radelet
Adrianne Sullivan-Campeau
Barbara Brooks Kimmel
Bob Pearson
Brian Grace
Chuck Wallington
Cy Wakeman
Frank Oswald
Gail Golden
Jean Lawrence
Jon Harris
Juan-Carlos Molleda
Ken Jacobs
Larry Krutchik
Linda Rutherford
Marta Ronquillo Newhart
Matt Ragas
Milagros Orcoyen
Pamela Meyer
Rob Metzger
Ron Culp
Samantha Stark
Samuel Hon
Soon Mee Kim
Steve Cody
Tina McCorkindale
Tom Watson

To our clients, past and present: Thank you for inviting us into your organizations and trusting us with your everyday and defining moments. Your willingness to grow and champion more authentic ways of leading has been the greatest teacher. The stories and insights within these pages exist because you've allowed me to learn alongside you. I'm profoundly grateful to the many supporters of our firm—the partners, colleagues, and advocates who have helped spread the message that how we communicate directly influences the cultures we create and the results we achieve.

To my friends who have supported me throughout this journey—thank you for your patience during the long hours of writing, for your honest feedback, and for reminding me why this work matters.

A special acknowledgment to my therapist, Breda, whose guidance helped me launch my journey of authenticity decades ago. That profound process of self-discovery fundamentally changed how I show up as a leader and as a person. I've come to believe that everyone needs a good coach—someone who can hold up a mirror, challenge our thinking, and help us see possibilities we might miss on our own. This kind of partnership is invaluable for any leader committed to growth.

Finally, to my family—Steve, Avi, and Noa—your love, support, and understanding have been my foundation. You've given me the space to pursue my passion while reminding me daily of what truly matters. The Heart First Leadership I write about was first learned and practiced at home with you.

As you turn these pages, my hope is that you'll find not just strategies and insights but also the encouragement that the heart work is worth it. In a world that often values metrics over meaning, remember that your greatest impact comes when you connect authentically with those you lead. The work of leadership isn't just about building organizations—it's about building people who then create something extraordinary together. Thank you for joining me on this journey.

With gratitude,

ACCLAIM FOR HEART WORK

"Everything about this book is exceptional! We come away from this, not just as better leaders but as better people. It's loaded with collective wisdom. Heart + Head; it's about time. Backed by data, with thoughtful insights to support it. It gives us a road map to build better organizations. A grand slam!"

—**Ric Bachrach,** CEO, Celebrity Focus, Inc.

"I've known David as an incredible leader who leads with heart and head. Now we have an indispensable guide to *how* to be that kind of a leader. From gratitude to listening to so much more, David unlocks the mystery of how to become the kind of leader you've always admired and aspired to be."

—**Roger Bolton,** Former CEO, Page

"David's Six Differentiators are to leadership what Porter's Five Forces are to strategy. I walked away with a new commitment to leading with gratitude and being an effective listener.

—**Stephen Smith,** Chairman, President & CEO, Amsted Industries

"In the same way David Grossman's latest book astutely connects strategic insights with human empathy, it maps the connection between a thriving workplace and a rewarding life. What leader wouldn't want to follow him there?"

—**Anthony D'Angelo,** APR, Fellow PRSA & Public Relations Department Chair & Professor of Practice, Syracuse University Newhouse School of Public Communications

"David Grossman is an icon, and now he has written one of the top leadership books to define success. His insights into gratitude, empathy, and communication provide a powerful playbook for leaders, from aspiring to seasoned."

—**Ray Day,** Vice Chair, Stagwell & Former CCO, IBM

"The best leaders don't just manage—they inspire. Grossman shows exactly how to create cultures of trust, innovation, and meaningful leadership."

—**Alim A. Dhanji,** CHRO, TD SYNNEX

"A must-read for any executive seeking to focus, inspire, and empower teams to meet the moment and more. David provides smart insights as to what it takes to be an effective leader today, supported by research, learning and planning tools, and practical advice from successful leaders."

—**Mike Fernandez,** Host of *The Crux of the Story* podcast & SVP of Public Affairs, Communications, and Sustainability, Enbridge

"Leadership is critical to every industry and sector. Leadership skills can be cultivated and applied at any age. David, drawing on his years of experience counseling corporate leaders and leading his own firm, provides keen insights to help professionals and youth to thrive. Thank you, David."

—**Rochelle Ford,** CEO, Page

"David's storytelling gets straight to the heart. He is clear and insightful. A must-read for anyone who wants to make a positive impact."

—**Andreas Frank,** CEO, Net32

"Inspiring, compelling, and refreshingly practical—a renewed sense of purpose and direction in a world where leadership is more challenging than ever."

—**Karmen Gardner,** VP, Corporate Communications & Employee Experience, Pella Corporation

"The best leaders know that numbers might reveal yesterday's results, but people create tomorrow's possibilities. *The Heart Work of Modern Leadership* beautifully illuminates what many of us miss—the gap between how empathetic we think we are and how our teams actually experience us. David doesn't just point out the problem; he also provides a practical road map for creating environments where people feel safe to speak truth and inspired to innovate. This is an essential guide for anyone serious about transforming their leadership impact in today's complex world."

—**Jennifer George,** SVP, Communications, The Aspen Group

ACCLAIM FOR HEART WORK

"*The Heart Work of Modern Leadership* offers a timely reminder that great leadership starts with understanding an organization's greatest asset: its people. David Grossman's insights reinforce the power of clear, empathetic, authentic, human-centered leadership."

—David Gitlin, Chairman & CEO, Carrier

"I loved everything about *The Heart Work of Modern Leadership*! It's clear, compelling, actionable, and deeply insightful. Whether you're leading a small team or a global organization, this book will change the way you lead."

—Jodi Glickman, CEO & Founder, Great on the Job

"David Grossman's insights have been invaluable to me as a CEO, board chair, and now as a mentor to senior leaders. His clear, memorable, and personal approach continues to resonate with every executive team I coach. *The Heart Work of Modern Leadership* distills what exceptional leaders actually do and why it matters, making it an essential read for anyone seeking to elevate their leadership.

—John J. Greisch, Chairman, Catalent, Inc.

"We're in a new era of leadership—one where only the most adaptable, human-centered leaders will thrive. This book offers a fresh and timely perspective on leading with both the head and the heart. Grounded in research and brought to life through the stories of respected leaders, it blends emotional intelligence with practical strategy. For leaders seeking to grow beyond their own experience, this is a vital and relevant resource."

—Aedhmar Hynes, Corporate Board Director, including Fluidra, Jackson Family Wines & IP Group, plc

"Grossman masterfully bridges leadership and communication, showing how the best leaders inspire, empower, and connect with their teams to drive real results."

—Bill Imada, Cofounder, Chairman & Chief Connectivity Officer, IW Group, Inc.

"David has done it . . . again. These new insights—based on experience, intelligence, instincts, and heart—are relevant, sensible, and (importantly) doable. They are critical to being a modern leader."

—Rich Jernstedt, President & CEO, The Jernstedt Company

"Grounded in new research and vivid stories, *The Heart Work of Modern Leadership* offers leaders a practical blueprint for balancing the head and heart. David Grossman shows how emotional intelligence, empathy, and creating a shared purpose can unleash human magic and fuel extraordinary results."

—**Hubert Joly,** Former Best Buy CEO, Senior Lecturer at Harvard Business School & Bestselling Author of *The Heart of Business*

"Strong and effective leadership is evolving, and *The Heart Work of Modern Leadership* provides today's busy leader with actionable takeaways to develop stronger teams and vibrant cultures within their organization. David delivers research-backed data and case studies from leaders who bring unique insights to the challenges facing all of us in an uncertain environment. This is a must-read for anyone who is committed to delivering results while being empathetic to those who we're entrusted to lead and serve."

—**Matthew Marcial,** CEO, Public Relations Society of America (PRSA)

"David Grossman's book arrives at a transition point in our world, when continuous disruption—technological, political, economic, societal, and environmental—is becoming the 'new normal.' This means leading organizations through constant change will be critical to enduring success. Leadership, not management, will determine the winners and losers. And because the younger generations of workers have different needs and expectations from the older employees, the emphasis this book puts on what used to be called 'soft skills' is spot on. Leading today's increasingly diverse, psychologically and emotionally attuned workers requires a different kind of leadership than was true in the 'my way or the highway' approach that was in vogue when I joined the workforce decades ago."

—**John Onoda,** Principal, iQ 360, Inc.

ACCLAIM FOR HEART WORK

"As a communications leader navigating today's complex and nuanced environment, I appreciated the six differentiators identified in this book. Specifically, leading with gratitude and taking the time to listen and empathize are key indicators of exceptional leadership. David elevates these critical human skills necessary for building trust and forging stronger connections to achieve impactful results."

—**Trity Pourbahrami,** Trustee of the Institute for Public Relations

"This book challenges the idea that leadership is only about business outcomes and reminds us it's also about emotional courage, context, and connection. David Grossman gives a modern playbook to lead with your heart, without losing your head."

—**Matt Prince,** Head of Brand Communications, KFC/Taco Bell

"The knowledge and teachings that David shares in this book are critical to anyone who aspires to be a better leader."

—**Dave Scholz,** CEO, Leger

"A game-changer for leaders looking to create engaged, high-performing teams. *The Heart Work of Modern Leadership* belongs on every executive's desk."

—**Michelle Russo,** CCO, State Farm

"David asserts that these times require leading with heart *in* head, and he provides the data, demonstrations, and detail to make the theory immediately actionable. He brings in a cadre of voices—all students of leadership in their professional roles—to add dimension to the concept."

—**Kim Sample,** President, PR Council

"This is a timely and wonderfully useful guide for any leader or aspiring leader who wants to crack the difficult code of human-centered leadership. Real-world examples plus David's beautifully articulated advice make this a book I know I will come back to often and share with my team."

—**Diane Schwartz,** CEO, Ragan

"*The Heart Work of Modern Leadership* offers a thoughtful framework for developing leadership behaviors that better reflect the realities of today's workforce. David Grossman provides practical, research-backed insights that can help bridge the gap between intent and impact—something every business leader and HR professional grapples with. The book is a useful resource for organizations working to align leadership development with evolving employee expectations."

—**Johnny C. Taylor Jr.,** President & CEO, Society for Human Resources Management (SHRM)

"Leadership is more than a cerebral exercise; it is a matter of the heart. Compassion, care, and investment are more important than what buttons to push to motivate employees. David has done a masterful job in this book of showing us what exceptional leadership does and should look like today!"

—**Damion Waymer,** Director, School of Journalism and Mass Communications, University of South Carolina

"This is the road map we've been waiting for. Leadership isn't about titles—it's about the choices we make, the courage we summon, and the humanity we refuse to lose. In *The Heart Work of Modern Leadership*, David Grossman puts language around what many of us feel but haven't quite articulated: that amid complexity and chaos, the best leaders are those who lead with both head and heart. As someone who believes that it's choice, not chance, that changes everything, I see this book as both mirror and map—a reflection of what leadership could be and a guide for how to rise to it. Grossman doesn't just diagnose what's broken—he delivers a deeply human blueprint for building workplaces where people can thrive, not just survive. This is heart work. And it's hard work. But it's also the only work that creates lasting impact."

—**Charlene Wheeless,** Speaker, Leadership Strategist & Bestselling Author

www.amplifypublishinggroup.com

The Heart Work of Modern Leadership: 6 Differentiators of Exceptional Leaders

Credit for author photo on cover flap: Heather Hackney Photography

For more information, please contact:
Amplify Publishing, an imprint of Amplify Publishing Group
620 Herndon Parkway, Suite 220
Herndon, VA 20170
info@amplifypublishing.com

Library of Congress Control Number: 2025925970

CPSIA Code: PRV1225A

ISBN-13: 979-8-90026-086-0

Printed in the United States

THE HEART WORK *of* MODERN LEADERSHIP

6 DIFFERENTIATORS *of* EXCEPTIONAL LEADERS

DAVID GROSSMAN

“

IT IS NOT WHAT WE THINK OR FEEL THAT MAKES US WHO WE ARE. IT IS WHAT WE DO. OR FAIL TO DO.

JANE AUSTEN

CONTENTS

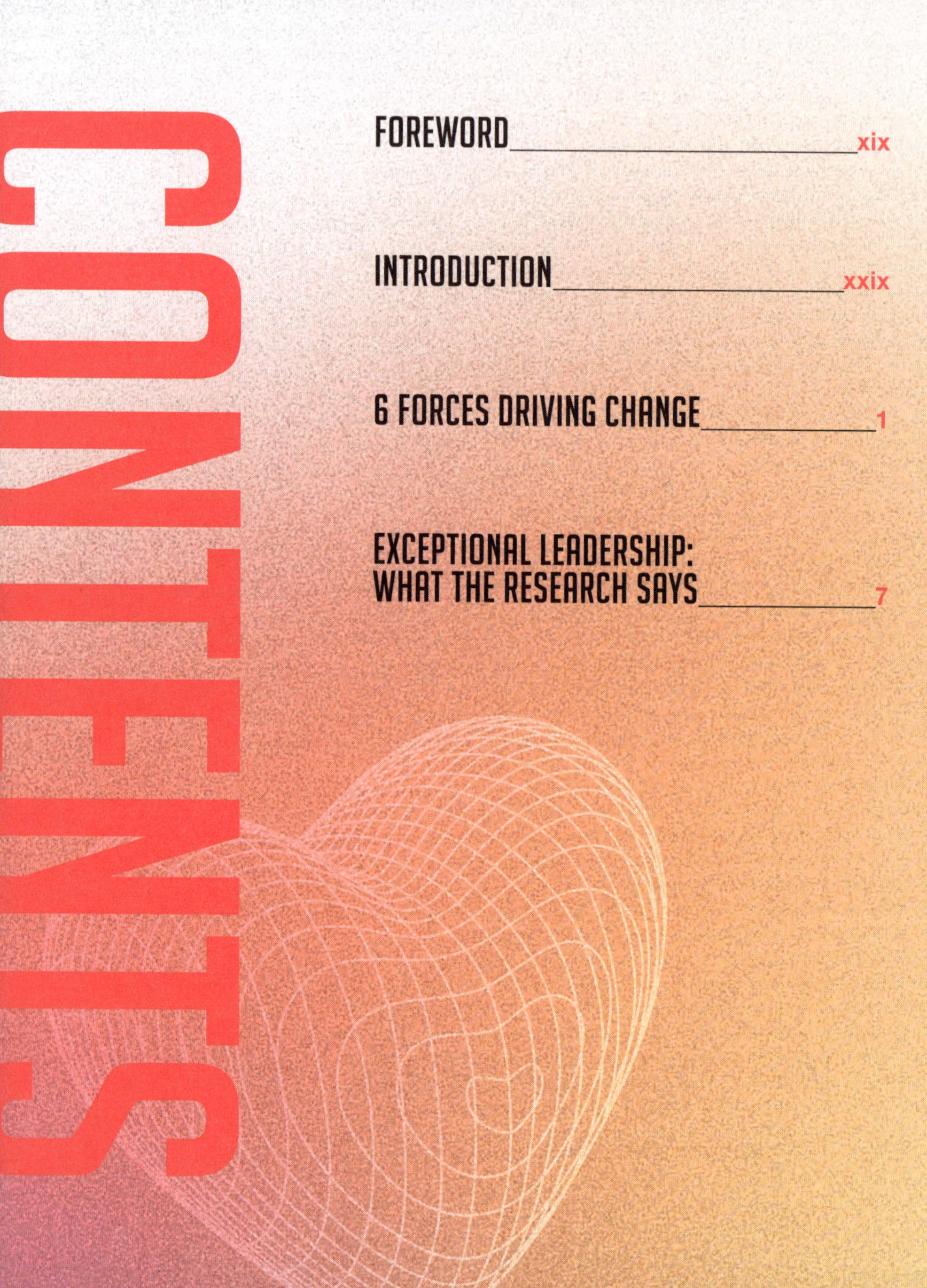

Throughout the book, meet these amazing modern leaders who exemplify what it means to lead with their heart in their head. Their experiences offer a rare glimpse into the real heart work of leadership—the tough decisions, the pivotal moments, and the unwavering commitment to their people. As you explore their insights, may you find inspiration, practical wisdom, and a renewed sense of what's possible in your own leadership journey.

PRO TIP: Just look for the blue gradient!

MY LEADERSHIP JOURNEY

is different than many of my peers. I never thought I would become a business leader, let alone the CEO of a major global company. It was never really a plan of mine. I'm from Norway and my father was from a humble background and had to become a sailor at the young age of 15. When he returned, he set up as an electrician, running this business with my mother. I was the first in my family to attend university, and after earning my degree, my father's advice was simple:

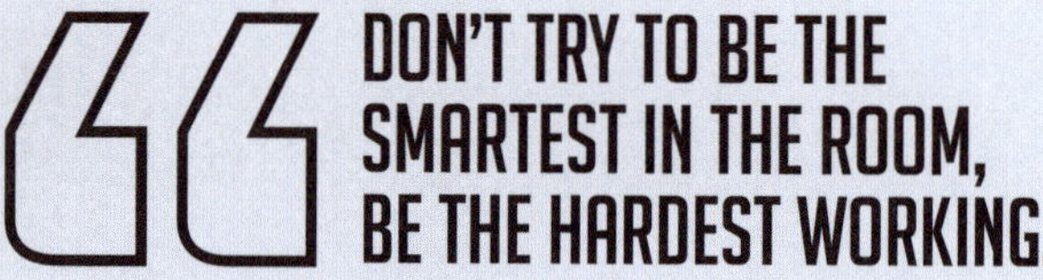

"DON'T TRY TO BE THE SMARTEST IN THE ROOM, BE THE HARDEST WORKING.

SVEIN TORE HOLSETHER
PRESIDENT & CEO, YARA INTERNATIONAL

AND SO ... I DID.

Grabbing every opportunity I could in my first finance role at a Norwegian metals and mining company. That hard work paid off—opening up many new opportunities for me, and I often used a highly analytical, data-driven approach in those early days.

Yet it wasn't long before I realized leadership was about a lot more than just working hard and having the right knowledge and expertise to make changes. I realized that even though I myself was a person driven by facts and figures, that's not necessarily the way you engage colleagues, drive enthusiasm, and promote teamwork. I knew I needed to get out of my comfort zone of logic and numbers and somehow reach people on a more personal and emotional level. Not the easiest task for an introvert.

It was only when I came to the realization that I didn't have to copy other CEOs, i.e., take on the appearance of what I thought a CEO should have, that things started happening. By finding a leadership style close to the person I am also in my private life—asking questions, being open about doubt and dilemmas, not having all the answers readily available—I think I was able to be authentic. The best thing about it is that when you don't pretend to be someone you're not, you're much more energy efficient.

In many ways, you can say that I learned how to apply the so-called "heart" piece to business in a more powerful way. That involved engaging the team on a personal level and earning their trust. It also meant thinking more deeply about the mission and purpose for employees and customers.

This combination of head and heart leadership came into clear focus in 2015, just after I was named CEO of Yara International, one of the world's leading fertilizer firms. Our company's key task is to help farmers across the world feed a global population of more than 8 billion people. Before coming on board, my most recent roles were in the aluminum industry. Yet as I read more about the company, I became increasingly intrigued with agriculture and the special responsibility this industry holds in feeding the world.

WHEN YOU DON'T PRETEND TO BE SOMEONE YOU'RE NOT, YOU'RE MUCH MORE ENERGY EFFICIENT.

At the time I assumed the CEO role, Yara was recovering from the reputational damage caused by a controversial corruption case, which had also taken its toll on our employees. I was determined to rebuild trust—both internally and externally—with our employees, our customers, and the global farming community.

As a first major step, I attended the 2015 United Nations Climate Conference in Paris. Immediately, I was incredibly impressed by the work of some of my fellow business leaders, discouraged by some other business leaders that were totally unprepared for the much-needed energy transition, and finally very inspired by the many youths who were championing the idea that business and government become far more active in sustainability and protecting the climate. The intensity and passion that I saw at that conference, especially from the youth protesters, left a lasting impression.

I realized then that Yara needed to revisit its own mission and vision and consider a much more active leadership role in sustainability and climate change. I also knew that it was not going to be an easy shift—and that my own executive board may not even agree immediately. After all, there's always a risk to being early or even a first mover. Yet from my point of view, it was a no-brainer. The world had already seen the consequences of climate change in 2015, and we knew this would be coming with even more force in the future. I decided then that it was worth the risk of making a bold change. In fact, I felt I would rather be fired for something I did than fired later for something I didn't do.

After the Paris Climate Conference, our team engaged with the whole organization for nearly a year circling in on our reason to exist as a company and recrafting our mission statement. Ultimately, we landed on a mission that pledges to responsibly feed the world and protect the planet. We have a growing population, and we need to produce more food for the world and achieve all of that with less emissions. There were some questions initially from Yara's board of directors about the new direction. One board member said, "All of the responsibility and sustainability points are valid, but in reality, when your operators come to work, isn't it really just about converting natural gas into fertilizer?" At that point, the head of our union interrupted, saying, "It's not that technical for us. We go to work because we want to create a product that helps feed the world."

It was a special moment for me to hear him share that. I honestly believe I can challenge the CEO of any company on our employees' ability to remember our mission statement and use it as a guiding star.

> “RESPONSIBLY FEED THE WORLD AND PROTECT THE PLANET.

I'm proud to say that Yara is on track for reducing its emissions; from 2005 to 2024 our emissions (scope 1 and 2) were down 50% and we're also focusing on producing lower carbon footprint fertilizers, made with carbon capture and storage or renewable sources rather than natural gas, which I believe will be a true game changer for our industry.

I've also joined global efforts with other business leaders promoting sustainability, because I believe we have an obligation to engage beyond our own balance sheets and work collaboratively through the whole value chain to find common ground. For me, the path we've been on at Yara isn't just rewriting the mission.

A big part of it was about engaging our teams along the way, with our hearts ***and*** our heads. I'm proud that our employees are inspired and helped us craft our mission, and I am committed to seeking and acting on their input in every way I can. One way I do that is by talking almost daily with the head of our employee union. He gives me great insights about what's really going on with the company. We're very much aligned and open to challenging each other when we aren't.

"HONEST EXCHANGES OF OPINIONS ARE CRUCIAL.

- REDUCING EMISSIONS
- INVESTING IN RENEWABLES
- CONNECTING WITH EMPLOYEES
- BUILDING TRUST

GAME CHANGER

Connecting with employees at all levels is one of the most important and enjoyable parts of my work. As a top leader, there is always the risk that you distance yourself too much or that people don't dare to be honest with you. Yet honest exchanges of opinions are crucial and with the union leaders especially, I can always count on them not sugarcoating it. I've found that we all want the same thing: to build long-term value for Yara. We have respect for each other's points of view and our relationship needs to **BE BUILT ON TRUST.**

200

250

150

I ALSO BELIEVE ONE OF THE BEST THINGS I CAN DO IS TO REPEATEDLY SHOW MY EMPLOYEES THROUGH CONCRETE ACTIONS JUST HOW MUCH I CARE AND HOW MUCH I PLAN TO LIVE OUT OUR VALUES EVERY DAY...

HOW DOES THIS FIT OUR PURPOSE?

One example of this is safety practices at Yara. To this day, I go through reportable accident reports every Friday afternoon, together with the line organization and the union. And I know every accident on a rolling 12-month basis by heart, so that I can go through every one and describe what happened. I know too well that knowledge can't be faked. I should be able to say what happened and I should be able to learn from that so we can avoid the same accidents in the future. I owe that to our employees and their friends and family members.

At Yara, we talk about our purpose every day. It is the foundation of everything we're doing. When in doubt about any decisions, we always ask, "How does this fit our purpose?" That came into play after Russia invaded Ukraine. Russia is a vital part of our food system, so we were cautious about imposing international economic sanctions against Russia that would impact the food supply in the short term. Yet we communicated strongly how to politically derisk from Russia's role in the food system in the long term. This is just one example of how our mission drives our policy decisions.

As I reflect back on my leadership journey over the years, I can honestly say that the balance of head and heart in my approach has guided me a lot and fueled successes we've achieved. Other leaders have also been really important in this context, Paul Polman being a particular inspiration and guide in those early days.

As we consider the many challenges we face in a world defined by a constant sense of crisis, I'm convinced this focus on head and heart—smart business practices coupled with genuine concern and respect for our employees and society—is the most essential ingredient for extraordinary leadership today. ■

LEADERS TODAY ARE FACING A PERFECT STORM

The demands on their time, their teams, and their own capacity seem to grow exponentially, while the pressure to deliver results has never been greater.

Fear not, good news is coming...

What's fascinating is that in my three decades of working with senior leaders across organizations of every size and industry, I see common themes emerge again and again—particularly in how the best leaders rise to meet these unprecedented challenges.

Yet, today's leadership landscape feels different. The demands of leaders have intensified in ways we've never seen before. Chances are, if you're reading this, you're feeling it. My guess is you're doing a lot of things right, but somehow, there's this nagging sense that good isn't quite good enough anymore. That's understandable, given the unprecedented time of change and complexity leaders navigate today.

Consider the short list: Increasing pressure for shareholder value. The rise of artificial intelligence. Lingering shifts in workplace expectations and the way we work, triggered by a global pandemic. Ongoing economic and political uncertainty around the world.

Recognizing the weight of those pressures on the leaders we work with, The Grossman Group partnered with The Harris Poll to get more clarity around what the workforce wants and needs most from its leaders now.

What Exceptional Leadership Looks Like Today

We wanted to understand what leaders and employees themselves would define as exceptional leadership versus "good" and "outdated" leadership. What we found is that employees have a very clear idea of what exceptional is—what Modern Leadership looks and feels like today.

Our study surveyed more than 2,206 employed Americans. The majority of employees graded their leaders as "good," with clear opportunities to elevate their impact and make a real difference in the engagement and motivation of their teams. A much smaller group put their leaders in the "exceptional" category, and 17% of employees said their leaders still used outdated, command-and-control leadership styles, leading to burnout, exhaustion, and disconnection.

What's super interesting—and the central focus of this book—is that the employees went on to define the specific actions that they believe sum up exceptional leaders. But first, here's a look at the overall report card.

Of the 2,206 employees surveyed, the leader grades lined up this way:

30%

OF LEADERS RATED "EXCEPTIONAL."

These leaders create environments where employees feel valued, supported, and able to do their best work.

54%

OF LEADERS RATED "GOOD."

While there are some positives to celebrate, these leaders have clear and critical opportunities to elevate their impact.

17%

OF LEADERS RATED "OUTDATED."

These leaders' approaches result in burnout, exhaustion, and disconnection.

As we share more details in this book, you'll see the themes of what it takes to be exceptional. It probably won't surprise you that the current workforce—fueled by a new generation looking for new kinds of leaders—craves more connection, meaning, and support than ever before. There's also no question that all employees, across generations, appreciate leaders open to greater flexibility and autonomy in how their employees work.

Achieving all that's asked of leaders is no small feat. At times, it may even feel like there's a personal cost for you as a leader, in your own stress levels, health impacts, and sense of well-being.

After all, the new business realities require an entirely different kind of leadership approach than what many of today's leaders experienced themselves. I think of my own career, including my time working part-time jobs in college and my early years in corporate communications. In those junior roles, there was little talk of my needs as an employee. My opinion was not often solicited. The whole idea of feeling heard and respected wasn't even part of the wider conversation. The exceptional leaders at that time asked for my perspective, and I felt seen, heard, and appreciated, but they were few and far between; more often, I just saw commands handed down.

While the culture has gradually changed, lingering effects of the old archetype remain, and plenty of leaders still try to emulate a command-and-control approach. In our survey alone, 17% of leaders were still placed in this category. Yet, when we and others ask employees, we get the same answer. The old approach isn't just outdated; it's actively harmful to both people and organizations.

To respond to the new needs, leaders are being asked to bring something much different to the modern workforce. That work isn't always easy, but I believe the path is absolutely worth it, and more achievable and fulfilling than it may seem. In many ways, the task ahead for leaders is about striking the right balance. Balance technological advancements, such as artificial intelligence, with human connection. Balance productivity with well-being and reasonable boundaries. Balance business results while also promoting personal growth for employees.

What Exactly Is a Modern Leader?

As our research with The Harris Poll uncovered, the short list of the character traits and habits that the workforce most admires in modern leaders includes six main leadership differentiators.

Where Do Heart and Head Fit In?

It is a classic debate in leadership circles today: What's most important—leading with your ***heart*** or your ***head?***

Characteristics:

- **Empathy:** Leaders prioritize understanding and connecting with their team members on an emotional level.
- **Relationship-Focused:** Leaders build strong relationships, and fostering a sense of belonging and loyalty among employees is paramount.
- **Values-Driven:** Decisions are often based on shared values and principles, promoting a positive workplace culture.
- **Encouragement:** Support and motivation are emphasized, creating an environment where employees feel valued and inspired.

Benefits:

- **Stronger Team Cohesion:** Emotional connections can lead to higher levels of trust and collaboration.
- **Increased Employee Satisfaction:** A caring approach can enhance morale and job satisfaction, reducing turnover.
- **Enhanced Creativity:** A supportive atmosphere encourages employees to share innovative ideas without fear of failure.

Challenges:

- **Decision-Making:** Relying too heavily on emotions may sometimes cloud judgment or lead to biased decisions.
- **Balancing Compassion and Accountability:** It can be challenging to maintain performance expectations while being empathetic.

My last book, *Heart First,* explored the many aspects of being more authentic in leadership and how that can profoundly inspire a team and move them to achieve remarkable things. So you may immediately see me as landing in the "heart" camp. Yet, that's one thing I wish I explained even better in *Heart First*. I don't believe leading with your heart means abandoning your head, or the logical, technical, and measurable skills leadership requires. Like most things that matter in leadership, the best leaders figure out how to do both very well while never neglecting either side of the equation. That's the kind of winning mindset that leaders need to strive for today.

Characteristics:

- **Logic and Analysis:** Leaders focus on data and metrics to guide decisions.
- **Strategic Thinking:** Emphasis is placed on long-term goals, vision, and systematic problem-solving.
- **Efficiency and Results:** Prioritization of productivity, performance metrics, and operational efficiency are key.
- **Risk Management:** Careful analysis of potential risks and consequences guide decision-making.

Benefits:

- **Clear Direction:** A logical approach can provide a clear roadmap for achieving goals.
- **Accountability:** Performance can be measured more easily, helping ensure that employees are meeting expectations.
- **Objective Decision-Making:** Relying on facts and data can reduce biases and lead to well-informed choices.

Challenges:

- **Potential Lack of Connection:** Focusing primarily on logic may result in a disconnect from employees' emotional needs.
- **Resistance to Change:** A rigid adherence to data may hinder adaptability and innovation within the team.

One example is leaders who get promoted into management because they deliver results. They might close deals, get products to customers on time after supply issues, and so on. Yet, when those leaders get into their new role, they may fail at the heart piece. This could be because they have their heads down and doors closed and are missing opportunities to demonstrate empathy and build relationships that set the right tone. These leaders often find that their technical skills take them only so far, and the heart skills are just as essential.

At the same time, there are other new leaders with off-the-chart "heart" skills, yet they lack the logic and analysis, strategic thinking, and risk management capabilities that allow them to carefully analyze the critical data needed to guide their decisions. They might rely too much on relationships alone and not enough on logic and results. They act impulsively, based on emotion rather than clear data. These leaders can easily fail, too.

"Heart First" does not mean we shy away from making tough business decisions when necessary. You can be a Heart First leader and still make tough calls, including restructuring, laying off employees, or having difficult conversations with team members about their performance. You can—and should—respectfully question or challenge team members at key moments to try better approaches or to push themselves to continually excel.

LEADING WITH YOUR HEART IN YOUR HEAD

Another way to think about Modern Leadership is to lead with your heart IN your head. Integrate emotional intelligence with strategic thinking. This requires both compassion and calculation, empathy and analysis. In practice, effective leaders blend both heart and head leadership:

- Making decisions that consider both the human impact and business objectives
- Seeing emotional intelligence as an essential skill (no longer a soft skill) and also as a strategic tool
- Approaching challenges with both analytical rigor and empathetic understanding
- Recognizing that care for people and organizational success are interdependent

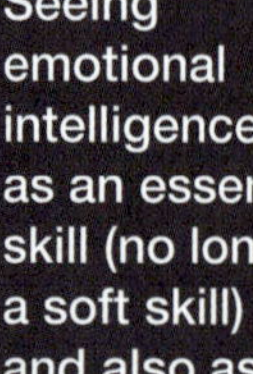

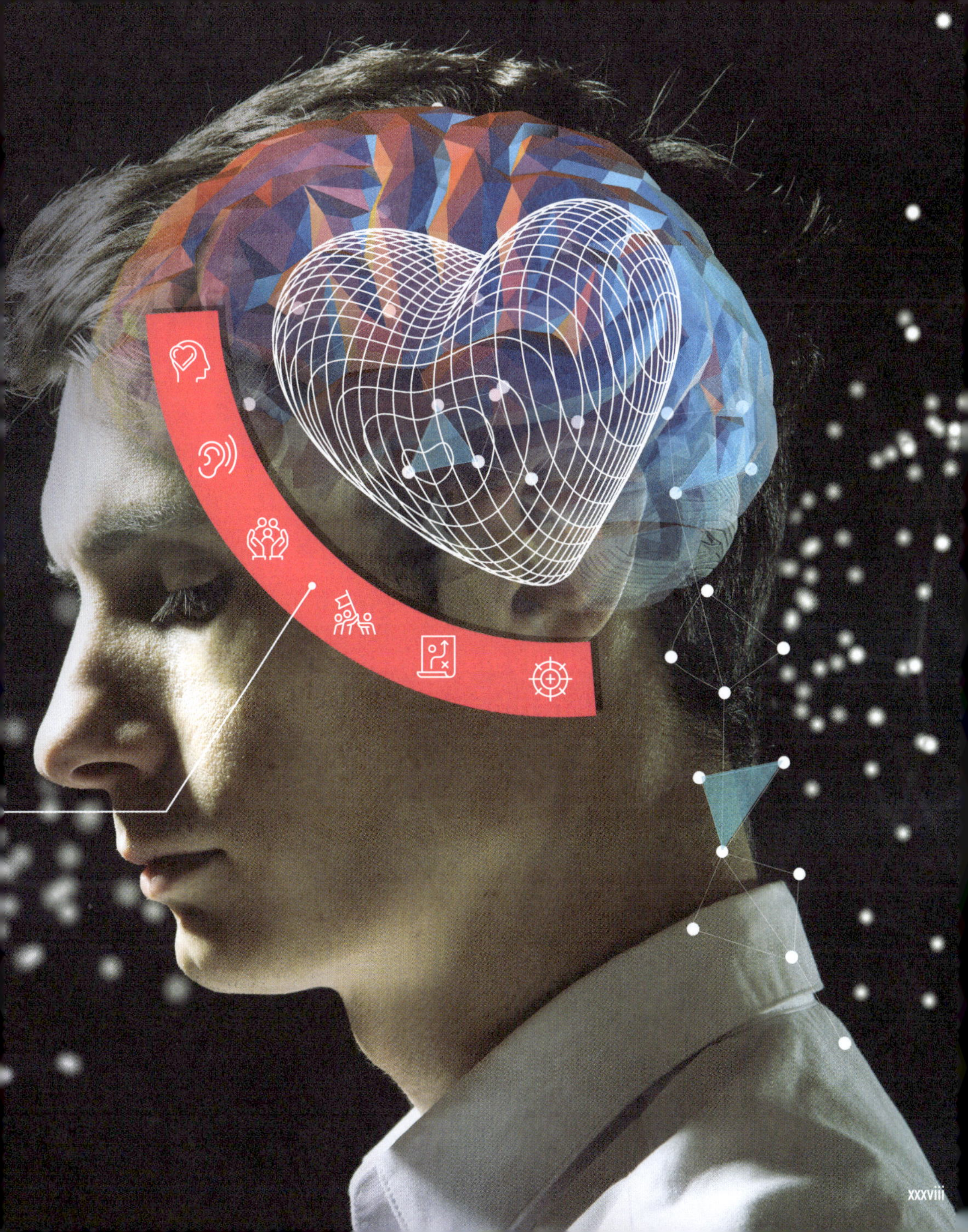

Modern leaders also know when to emphasize one style over the other, adapting their approach based on the needs of their team, and the demands of the situation and the business.

Head & Heart

It makes sense then that the best leaders need both, and pretty much in equal measure. Balancing emotional intelligence with analytical thinking can create a more holistic leadership approach that drives both employee engagement and organizational success. In this way, leadership becomes a double whammy of emotional intelligence and a rational mindset. When leaders work with this kind of humility—thinking like a scientist in search of the best solutions—they ask great questions, facilitate collaboration, and build a team culture that is noticeably open and innovative. This is where the magic happens, and how the greatest companies are made.

What It Takes to Move from Good to Exceptional

Our research with The Harris Poll also identified insightful patterns for how leaders move from good to exceptional. From that work, we've pinpointed seven elements to serve as the guideposts for Modern Leadership:

GRATITUDE	CULTURE	FIT
Show gratitude, acknowledging hard work and effort.	Create a culture where employees want to come to work and be at their best.	Help employees know how they fit into the company's long-term talent strategy.

LISTENING	EMPATHY	ACCOUNTABILITY	WELL-BEING
Listen more closely to employees and stakeholders to truly understand.	Demonstrate empathy in a variety of ways.	Lead by example and be personally accountable.	Champion well-being across the organization, and with intention.

Why Moving from Good to Great Matters

The positive news from our research is that many employees rated their leaders as "good" right now. So, what's the problem? For some, good may feel like good enough. Yet, as Jim Collins' famous *Good to Great* business management book argued, moving from good to great is everything. Many of the companies Collins profiled in 2001 would have failed in the long run had they not taken action to pursue excellence at that time. The same is true for leaders. When we don't push ourselves beyond the status quo, ultimately, we limit our own potential, and that of our teams.

I've seen this in our own work and the work of our clients. Many of the business leaders who contributed to this book have seen it too. One leader at CareRX Canada shared that the organization tracks employee retention monthly. When retention seriously slides and new leaders are brought in, the results are clear: retention improves, employees feel supported, and engagement goes up.
This is just one example that shows that the way leaders lead truly matters.

The practices we lay out in more detail in this book serve as a blueprint for the kinds of actions that make a lasting difference for leaders and the companies they lead. Employees are craving modern leaders who are up to the task. Let us help you get on track with the transformative heart work of Modern Leadership.

Making the Most of *The Heart Work of Modern Leadership*

This book was specifically designed for you—the busy leader. It's structured to serve you in multiple ways, depending on your time, immediate leadership challenges, and development goals. While reading cover-to-cover provides the complete journey of exceptional leadership, there are several ways to extract immediate value:

For Immediate Impact: When facing a specific leadership challenge, use the detailed table of contents to jump directly to the differentiator you want to focus on or other relevant sections. Each section is crafted to stand alone while fitting into the larger transformation journey needed, and includes actionable insights for senior leadership teams and those who advise them.

Research Highlights: Every chapter starts with "What the Research Says," grounding you in the latest, greatest data on the topic.

Articles: Every article is designed as a self-contained lesson with some purposeful repetition from article to article. Some articles address the same topic in different ways, and with varying suggestions, allowing you to pick and choose what might work best for you.

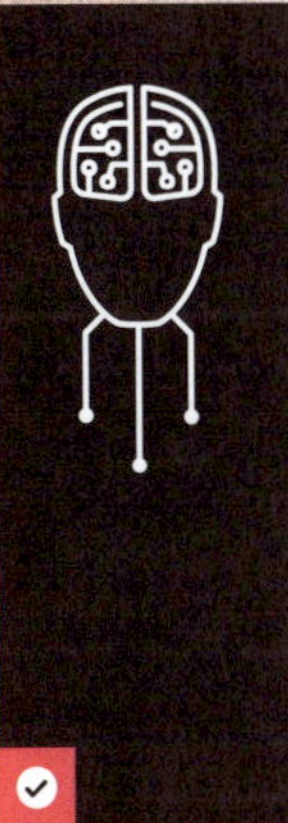

Learning Devices: Throughout the book, you'll find several learning tools to deepen your understanding:

- Reflection Questions that help you apply concepts to your leadership context.
- Action Guides with specific steps for implementation.
- "What It Sounds Like" examples that provide practical language.
- Common Pitfalls to Avoid sections that help you avoid typical mistakes.
- Real-world case studies illustrating key concepts.

Quick Reference Tools: Many chapters contain some of our most-used tools by leaders like yourself.

Development Planning: Many sections include 30-, 60-, and 90-day implementation plans, helping you systematically transform concepts into practice. These structured approaches help you build new leadership habits over time.

For ongoing development, consider keeping the book easily accessible and referring to it regularly as different leadership challenges arise. Remember: This isn't just a book to be read—it's a leadership toolkit to be used. Whether you have 5 minutes or 5 hours, you can find valuable insights and practical strategies to bring out the modern leader in you. ■

6 FORCES DRIVING CHANGE

No doubt, we're living in an era of unprecedented change and complexity. A number of forces have accelerated the need for Modern Leadership.

1 WORKPLACE TRANSFORMATION

The workplace upheaval of 2020-2023 revealed a profound shift in what employees seek from their leaders and organizations. When traditional playbooks fell short during the pandemic, successful leaders discovered the power of authenticity and empathy. One executive shared with me, "We had no roadmap—we simply had to be human." This insight became a guiding principle for leadership moving forward.

Today's employees seek more than competitive compensation or traditional benefits. They want leaders who demonstrate genuine understanding of their challenges, celebrate their contributions, and create opportunities for growth. This means providing meaningful flexibility in how work happens, showing clear connections between daily tasks and organizational purpose, and fostering environments where career development is prioritized.

As leaders, we must recognize this isn't a temporary adjustment but a fundamental transformation in how we engage and retain talent. Our role is to create cultures where team members feel truly valued, empowered to contribute meaningfully, and supported in their professional journey. The most successful leaders balance empathy with execution, blending Heart First Leadership with clear business focus. When we lead this way, we build the trust and engagement needed for sustainable success.

2 MENTAL HEALTH AWARENESS AND WORKPLACE WELLNESS

The pandemic highlighted the critical importance of supporting employee well-being. Remote work has blurred traditional boundaries, while ongoing uncertainty contributes to stress and burnout. Forward-thinking leaders recognize that creating psychologically safe environments where teams can openly discuss challenges isn't just compassionate—it's essential for sustainable performance.

And check-ins aren't just about work; they also focus—in part or exclusively at times—on how the employee is managing their mental health and well-being.

3 GENERATIONAL EXPECTATIONS

Millennials and Gen Zers, who now make up the majority of our workforce, are fundamentally reshaping leadership expectations. These generations seek more than just career advancement—they want work that aligns with their personal values and contributes to a better world. These team members value continuous feedback and growth opportunities, preferring regular coaching conversations over annual reviews.

They expect leaders to share the context behind decisions and welcome their input on issues affecting their work. Most importantly, they seek leaders who demonstrate self-awareness, acknowledge their own growth areas, and create psychologically safe environments where authentic dialogue thrives.

For leaders, this means moving beyond traditional hierarchical relationships to become more accessible mentors and coaches. We must invest time in understanding individual aspirations, provide meaningful growth opportunities, and create clear connections between daily work and the larger organizational purpose.

4 SOCIAL JUSTICE AWARENESS

The global focus on equity has fundamentally changed what employees expect. Our teams want to see meaningful action behind organizational statements and that they're tied to the organization's purpose and values.

They also look for leaders who actively seek out diverse perspectives, address unconscious bias, and create environments where everyone can bring their evolved selves to work.

This requires leaders to examine their own assumptions and blind spots while building cultural competence. Modern leaders create forums for honest dialogue about challenging topics, ensuring all voices are heard and valued.

Effective leaders recognize that inclusion isn't a program—it's a mindset that shapes every decision, from hiring and development to how we run meetings and recognize contributions.

5 ECONOMIC UNCERTAINTY

Market volatility and economic pressures create layers of stress for our teams that extend far beyond the workplace. Employees worry about job security, retirement savings, and providing for their families. Many face complex financial pressures, supporting adult children or aging parents while managing their own financial well-being.

The need then is regular, transparent updates about business performance and organizational health, while creating opportunities for open dialogue about economic concerns. Modern leaders ensure teams know about available financial wellness resources and benefits, while maintaining focus on career development to enhance job security.

Most importantly, they recognize and reward contributions consistently, showing employees they're valued even in challenging times.

6 AI AND AUTOMATION ANXIETY

The acceleration of artificial intelligence and automation creates natural concerns about job security and workplace transformation. Employees question their future roles, wonder which skills they'll need, and seek clarity about how their work will evolve.

As leaders, we must help our teams navigate this transition thoughtfully through transparent communication about technological changes and their timeline. This means working with each team member to create development plans that focus on future-ready skills, while showing how AI and automation can enhance rather than replace human work. Most importantly, we must continually reinforce the enduring value of uniquely human skills like creativity, emotional intelligence, and complex problem-solving.

WHAT AI CAN'T DO:
The Power of Human Leadership

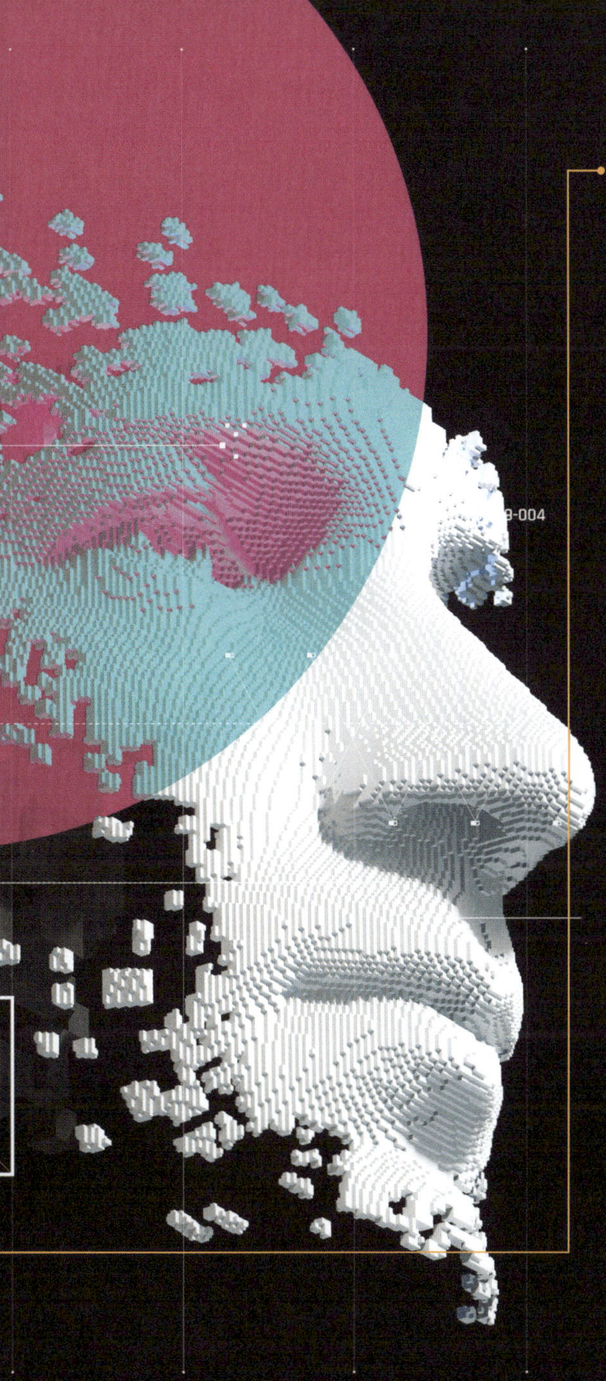

Leaders today bring irreplaceable human qualities that AI simply cannot replicate.

True Empathy and Emotional Intelligence: Understanding and managing our own emotions while genuinely connecting with others' feelings and experiences.

Vision Creation and Inspiration: Crafting compelling futures that motivate teams to achieve more than they thought possible.

Complex Relationship-Building: Navigating intricate interpersonal dynamics and resolving conflicts with wisdom and care.

Cultural Understanding: Respecting and embracing diverse perspectives while fostering authentic inclusion across teams.

Ethical Decision-Making: Facing difficult choices that require principled judgment, lived experience, and a deep understanding of human values.

Culture Shaping: Instilling meaningful values and rallying people around shared purpose in ways that transform organizations.

Authentic Mentorship: **Providing nuanced guidance, support, and encouragement that helps others grow and thrive.**

EXCEPTIONAL LEADERSHIP: WHAT THE RESEARCH SAYS

What does it take to be an exceptional leader today? The Grossman Group/Harris Poll study offers a clear roadmap for any leader hoping to stand apart and help employees thrive in an age of unprecedented change and disruption in business.

Surveying 2,206 employed Americans over two waves in mid-2024, our study reveals that becoming an exceptional leader is absolutely achievable when leaders focus on a core set of essential skills.

The study groups leaders into three main categories: exceptional, good, and outdated. Among our most important findings is that only 30% of leaders were defined as exceptional and meeting the evolving needs of today's workforce. We also identify a sizable gap between what employees define as merely "good" and "exceptional."

The differences in employee experience under each of the leadership categories are striking. Under exceptional leaders, employees consistently report feeling valued, appreciated, and that their work matters. In stark contrast, those working under outdated leadership are far more likely to feel burnt out, exhausted, and overwhelmed.

Here's a breakdown of the three distinct categories of leadership identified by employees:

30%

EXCEPTIONAL LEADERS

These leaders create environments where employees feel valued, supported, and able to do their best work.

54%

GOOD LEADERS

While somewhat positive, these leaders have important opportunities to elevate their impact to stand out and motivate and engage their teams.

17%

OUTDATED LEADERS

These leaders' approaches are more top-down and less collaborative. They result in burnout, exhaustion, and disconnection from employees.

Methodology Overview

Research

- The objective of this research was to gauge what Exceptional Leadership looks like today in America, positioned next to Good Leadership and Outdated Leadership for senior leaders.
- N=2,206 Employed Americans
  - Fielded by The Harris Poll over two waves:
    - June 18–21, 2024
    - July 9–11, 2024
  - All data weighted to US Census
  - Analyzed and synthesized into this study by The Harris Poll

Key Groups

- **Exceptional Leadership respondents:** These respondents have self-reported that the Senior Leadership at their company is "Exceptional."
  - n=655
- **Good Leadership respondents:** These respondents have self-reported that the Senior Leadership at their company is "Good."
  - n=1,187
- **Outdated Leadership respondents:** These respondents have self-reported that the Senior Leadership at their company is either "Mediocre" or "Poor."
  - n=364

How Employees Feel

A critical finding from the research is that how leaders lead clearly impacts how employees feel about their work. Here's how employees feel when they are led by an exceptional, good, and outdated leader:

EXCEPTIONAL FEELS LIKE ...

- I feel like what is important to me is valued
- I feel valued and appreciated
- I feel I am reaching my full potential

GOOD FEELS LIKE ...

- I feel like I am making a positive impact
- I feel that my work matters
- I feel a sense of belonging

OUTDATED FEELS LIKE ...

- I feel overwhelmed
- I feel exhausted
- I feel burnt out
- I feel bored

HEART
LEAD WITH GRATITUDE
FOSTER AN INCLUSIVE CULTURE
LISTEN AND EMPATHIZE
6
DIFFERENTIATORS
OF MODERN LEADERSHIP
CONNECT STRATEGY TO EMPLOYEE GROWTH
ENABLE EMPLOYEES TO MEET THE MOMENT
COMMUNICATE WITH CONTEXT
HEAD

DEFINED

1. LEAD WITH GRATITUDE

SEE PAGE 25

Exceptional leaders are **8.2 times better** at expressing genuine appreciation compared to outdated leaders. They make gratitude a daily practice, not an occasional gesture.

What It Means:

Senior Leadership...

- Shows gratitude to employees, acknowledging hard work and effort
- Creates a culture where employees want to come to work and be at their best
- Promotes the importance of employees focusing on personal well-being, including both mental and physical well-being

Why It Matters:

54% of employees working under exceptional leaders strongly agree that their leaders show gratitude and acknowledge hard work. Only 5% of those under outdated leaders report the same. This is the largest performance gap among all leadership differentiators.

2. LISTEN AND EMPATHIZE

SEE PAGE 53

The research shows exceptional leaders are **6.9 times better** than outdated leaders at demonstrating genuine empathy and understanding. They create safe spaces for feedback and vulnerability.

What It Means:

Senior Leadership...

- Listens to understand
- Fosters a sense of unity across departments and teams—recognizing that everyone is working towards a common goal
- Shows empathy with employees
- Creates an environment where individuals feel safe to share feedback, take risks, and be vulnerable in front of one another
- Creates an environment where employees feel valued and understood

Why It Matters:

51% of employees strongly agree that their leaders make an effort to listen to understand; 48% say their leaders show empathy (compared to 21% under good leaders); and 47% say their leaders create environments where employees feel valued and understood (compared to 6% under outdated leaders).

3. FOSTER AN INCLUSIVE CULTURE

SEE PAGE 89

Creating an environment where employees want to come to work and be at their best is a hallmark of exceptional leadership, with these leaders performing **7.09 times better** than outdated leaders in this area.

What It Means:

Senior Leadership…

- Works to understand the unique backgrounds and experiences of employees to improve culture
- Leads by example and is accountable for their actions
- Demonstrates a focus on building trust with employees
- Finds space for creativity and injects it into everyday activities

Why It Matters:

45% of employees strongly agree that senior leadership creates an environment where individuals feel safe to share feedback, take risks, and be vulnerable in front of one another. This compares to just 7% of employees reporting those feelings when working for an outdated leader.

4. COMMUNICATE WITH CONTEXT

SEE PAGE 133

Top leaders are **7.28 times more effective** than outdated leaders at adjusting their communication to meet employee needs. They're intentional about consistently communicating strategy and ensuring transparency.

What It Means:

Senior Leadership...

- Calibrates their communication to meet employee needs
- Communicates with transparency
- Acts on employee feedback

Why It Matters:

46% of employees under exceptional leaders strongly agree that their leaders communicate with transparency, and 44% report intentional and consistent communication of company strategy.

5. CONNECT STRATEGY TO EMPLOYEE GROWTH

SEE PAGE 171

Top leaders excel at helping employees understand how they fit into the company's long-term vision, performing **6.36 times better** than outdated leaders in this area.

What It Means:

Senior Leadership...

- Helps employees know how they fit in the company's long-term talent strategy
- Consistently communicates company strategy
- Involves employees in company change
- Ensures communication is focused on helping employees understand why change is needed and how it will help the organization evolve
- Demonstrates that people are the greatest investment and finds traditional or creative ways to support employee development

Why It Matters:

46% of employees working for exceptional leaders strongly agree that senior leaders help employees know how they fit into the company's long-term talent strategy. This compares to just 5% for employees under outdated leaders.

6. ENABLE EMPLOYEES TO MEET THE MOMENT

SEE PAGE 197

Exceptional leaders are **8.04 times more likely** to actively support employee development and provide resources for growth compared to outdated leaders.

What It Means:

Senior Leadership...

- Actively exposes individuals to best practices and bold ideas to meet the moment of today
- Understands the work that needs to be done and selects the right people for those roles
- Encourages collaboration across the organization and creates avenues for this to occur
- Is able to successfully deploy new tech that positively impacts workload and culture
- Ensures employees understand how their work connects to the purpose of the organization

Why It Matters:

45% of employees working under exceptional leaders strongly agree their leaders demonstrate that people are the greatest investment and find traditional or creative ways to support employee development. Only 4% of employees working for outdated leaders report this.

The Heart-Head Leadership Balance

One of the most fascinating insights from the research is that while both "heart" and "head" leadership traits matter, heart-centered leadership qualities have an edge in driving exceptional results. As the following chart highlights, **nine out of the top 10 traits of exceptional leaders are heart-focused.**

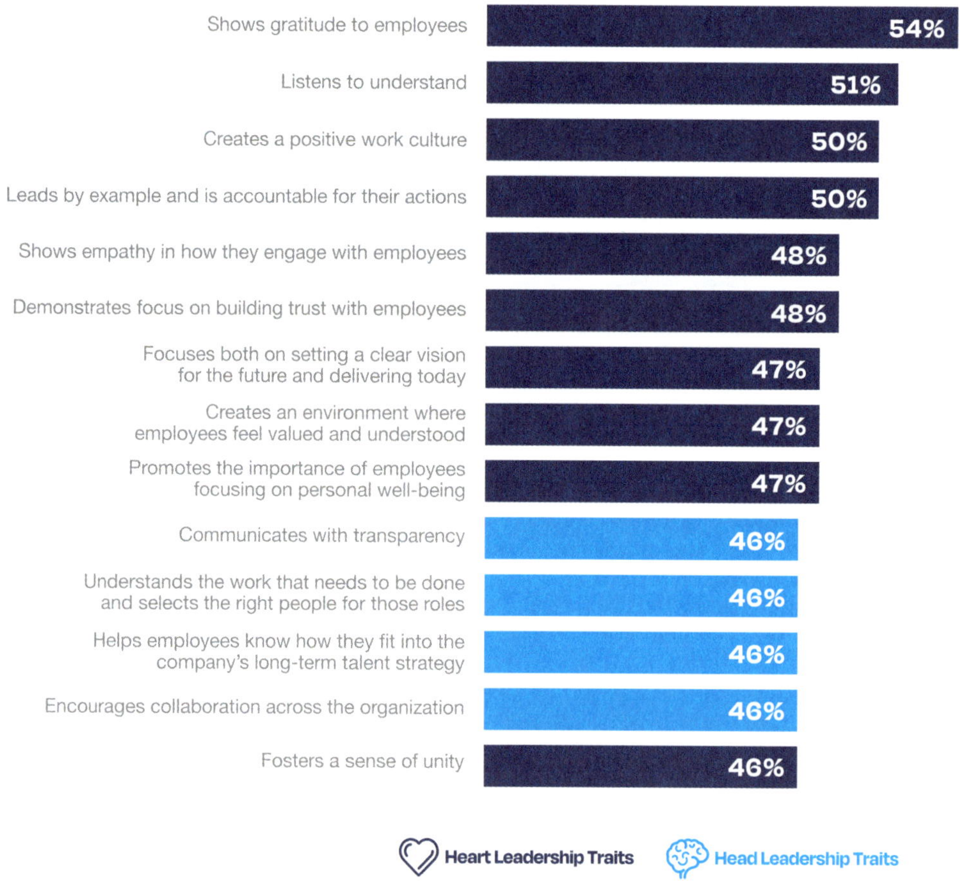
Shows gratitude to employees
54%
Listens to understand
51%
Creates a positive work culture
50%
Leads by example and is accountable for their actions
50%
Shows empathy in how they engage with employees
48%
Demonstrates focus on building trust with employees
48%
Focuses both on setting a clear vision for the future and delivering today
47%
Creates an environment where employees feel valued and understood
47%
Promotes the importance of employees focusing on personal well-being
47%
Communicates with transparency
46%
Understands the work that needs to be done and selects the right people for those roles
46%
Helps employees know how they fit into the company's long-term talent strategy
46%
Encourages collaboration across the organization
46%
Fosters a sense of unity
46%
Heart Leadership Traits
Head Leadership Traits

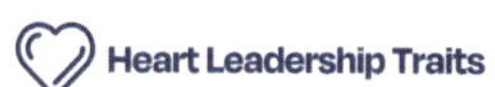

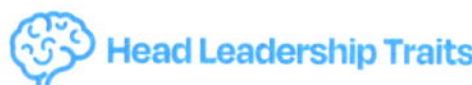

Q: *Please indicate how much you agree or disagree with the following phrases as it pertains to Senior Leadership at your current position with your primary employer.*

Our key takeaway from this is that the best leaders know how to lead with both their

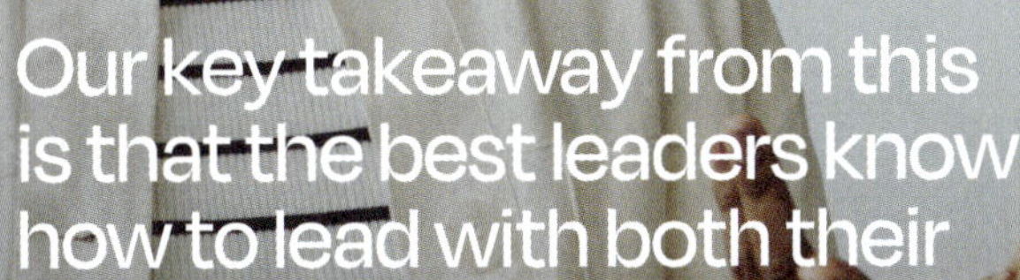

finding many opportunities to integrate both elements into their leadership style.

The Costs of Outdated Leadership

The research also provides an important warning about the costs of outdated leadership approaches. Employees feel lousy under outdated leaders. As we have highlighted, employees frequently report feeling burnt out, exhausted, overwhelmed, bored, and under a constant sense of pressure when working for outdated leaders. Employees feel outdated leaders have the wrong priorities, strongly agreeing with the following statements:

38%
say leadership is more concerned with external stakeholders than employee well-being

37%
report leadership is absent in helping build positive workplace culture

32%
feel leadership focuses on short-term wins over long-term success

EXCEPTIONAL

The gap between exceptional and outdated leadership is particularly stark in three areas:

Investing in people and finding ways to support employee development

11.3X
Difference

Showing gratitude and acknowledging hard work

10.8X
Difference

Demonstrating its focus on building trust with employees

9.6X
Difference

OUTDATED

The Path from Good to Exceptional

Our research identifies a notable gap between good and exceptional leaders. Employees also reported seven leadership elements that define what it means to be exceptional. This is what we consider the clear roadmap for how leaders can move from good to exceptional. Here's a snapshot of the seven elements that define great leaders, and the chasm that good leaders need to cross to become exceptional.

Essential Elements on the Path to Great:	EXCEPTIONAL LEADERS	GOOD LEADERS	
	STRONGLY AGREE	STRONGLY AGREE	THE GAP
Gratitude: Senior leadership shows gratitude to employees, acknowledging hard work and effort	54%	25%	29%
Culture: Senior leadership creates a culture where employees want to come to work and be at their best	50%	21%	29%
Fit: Senior leadership helps employees know how they fit into the company's long-term talent strategy	46%	19%	27%
Listening: Senior leadership listens to understand	51%	24%	27%
Empathy: Senior leadership shows empathy in how they engage with employees	48%	21%	27%
Accountability: Senior leadership leads by example and is accountable for their actions	50%	23%	27%
Well-Being: Senior leadership promotes the importance of employees focusing on personal well-being, including both mental and physical well-being	47%	20%	27%

WHERE WE GO FROM HERE

What we learn from this research is that exceptional leadership is strongly felt by employees. They know a great leader when they're fortunate enough to work for one. Employees also paint a clear picture of how leaders can become exceptional. This is the topic we'll focus on for the remainder of this book, helping you see how you can implement the six exceptional leadership differentiators into your daily work.

What's most encouraging about these leadership differentiators is how specific—and doable—they are in practice. Striving to implement these approaches is well worth the effort. Our research shows that making the shift from good to exceptional creates measurable improvements in employee engagement, reduces burnout, and drives organizational success. Our employees are asking for better from modern leaders.

NOW'S THE TIME FOR ALL OF US TO MEET THE MOMENT.

1. LEAD WITH GRATITUDE

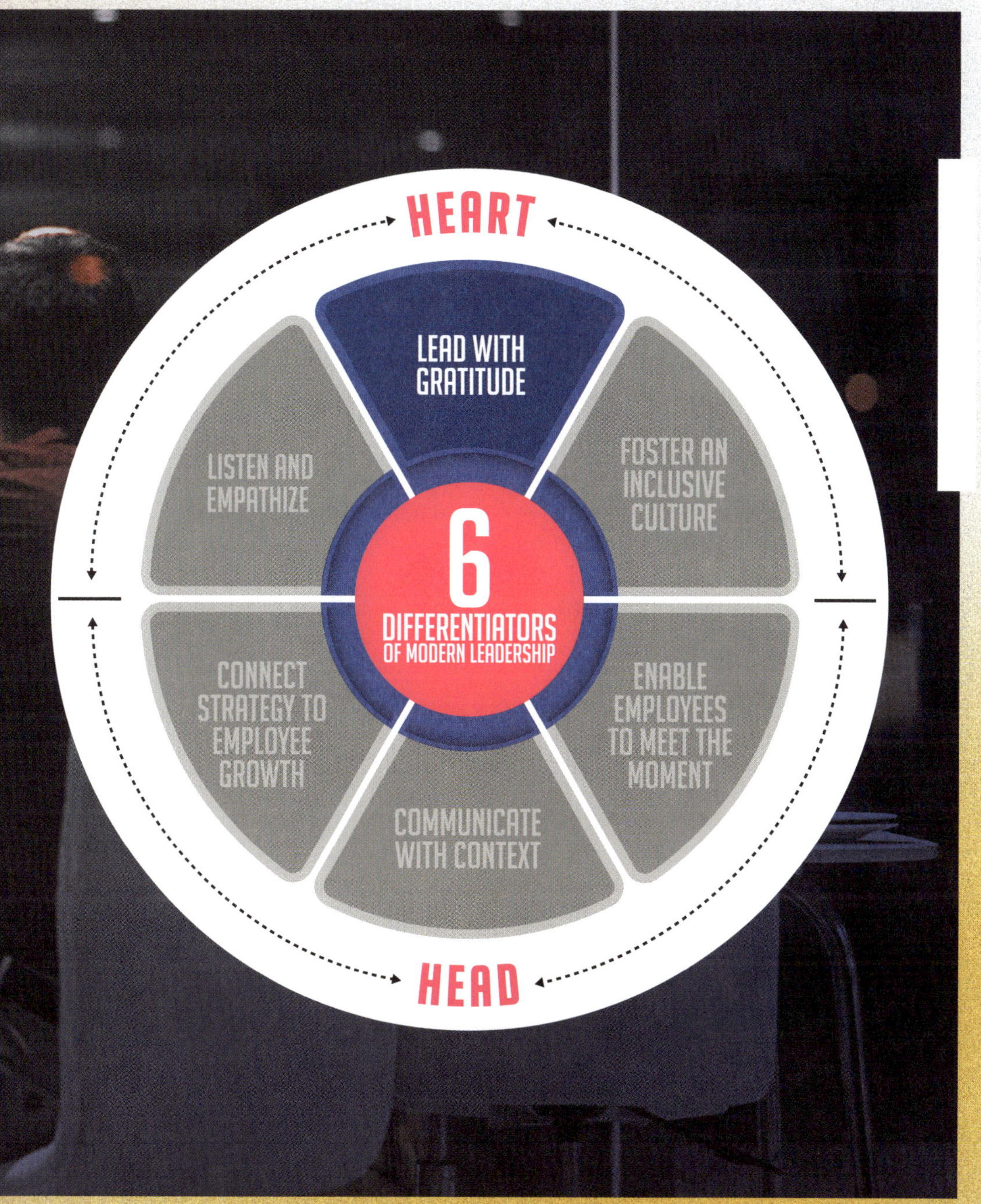
HEART
LEAD WITH GRATITUDE
FOSTER AN INCLUSIVE CULTURE
ENABLE EMPLOYEES TO MEET THE MOMENT
COMMUNICATE WITH CONTEXT
CONNECT STRATEGY TO EMPLOYEE GROWTH
LISTEN AND EMPATHIZE
6
DIFFERENTIATORS
OF MODERN LEADERSHIP
HEAD

GRATITUDE isn't just a "nice to have" leadership trait—it's a business imperative and the foundation upon which all other leadership success is built. It supports psychological safety, which enables innovation. It builds trust that accelerates change. It demonstrates empathy that drives engagement. In short, gratitude is the catalyst that transforms good leadership into exceptional leadership.

I've seen firsthand how teams transform when leaders make genuine appreciation a cornerstone of their approach. Teams become more innovative, change happens more smoothly, and results accelerate dramatically.

Yet, despite these clear benefits, many leaders still struggle to make gratitude a consistent part of their leadership style. Some worry it might diminish their authority. Others simply don't know how to express appreciation in ways that feel authentic and meaningful. And in today's fast-paced business environment, taking time to show gratitude can feel like a luxury we can't afford. The reality? We can't afford not to.

This chapter explores how to lead with gratitude in practical, actionable ways. You'll discover proven strategies for making appreciation a natural part of your leadership style, creating a culture where employees want to be at their best, and ensuring that employees are taking care of their well-being, both mental and physical.

The journey to exceptional leadership begins with a simple "thank you"—but it's how we express that thanks, when we share it, and what we make a priority that makes the difference. Let's explore how to make gratitude not just something we do but a fundamental part of who we are as leaders.

WHAT THE RESEARCH SAYS

IMPLEMENTING GRATITUDE IN THE WORKPLACE CAN **significantly improve** EMPLOYEES' MENTAL WELL-BEING, ENGAGEMENT, AND JOB SATISFACTION.[1]

EMPLOYEES WHO RECEIVE RECOGNITION AT LEAST MONTHLY ARE **2.6 times more likely** TO REPORT BEING HIGHLY ENGAGED AT WORK COMPARED TO THOSE RECOGNIZED ANNUALLY OR LESS.[2]

SOURCE

[1] Harty B, Gustafsson JA, Thorén M, Möller A, Björkdahl A. Development of a gratitude intervention model and investigation of the effects of such a program on employee well-being, engagement, job satisfaction and psychological capital.

[2] Nobes, Caitlin. 2024 State of Recognition: Optics vs Impact. Achievers Workforce Institute.

GRATITUDE HAS **significant impacts** ON MORAL, RELATIONAL, AND WELLNESS OUTCOMES FOR BOTH BENEFICIARIES AND BENEFACTORS.[3]

PEOPLE WHO REGULARLY PRACTICE GRATEFUL THINKING CAN INCREASE THEIR "SET POINT" FOR HAPPINESS BY AS MUCH AS

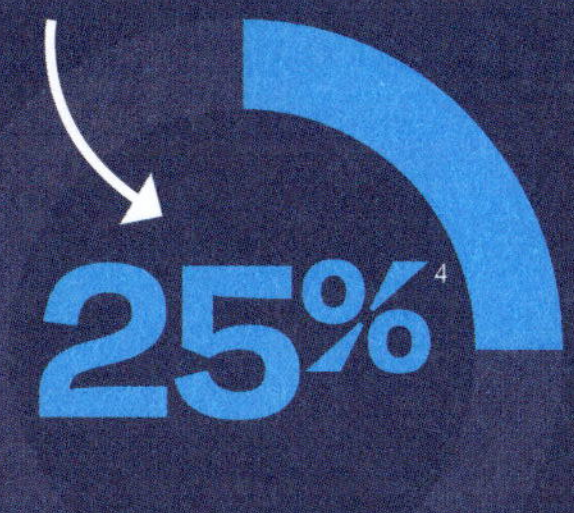

[3]Locklear, L. R., Sheridan, S., & Kong, D. T. (2023). Appreciating social science research on gratitude: An integrative review for organizational scholarship on gratitude in the workplace. Journal of Organizational Behavior, 44(2), 225-260.

[4]Emmons, R. A. (2007). Thanks!: How the new science of gratitude can make you happier. Houghton Mifflin Harcourt.

01

PUT ON YOUR O_2 MASK BEFORE ASSISTING THOSE AROUND YOU

We pride ourselves on producing groundbreaking work. Think about the last time you did that—how great it felt, the energy and focus you had. Now, consider the circumstances that made it possible. Chances are, you were in a good state of mind—and likely a good state of body as well.

As leaders, our job is to maximize the number of times our teams are in a position to do exceptional work. And the most effective way to do that is by modeling the behavior ourselves.

When I was a reporter, I made a habit of swimming before work. I'd walk into the newsroom energized, happy, and ready to take on the world. That's when I first realized the direct impact fitness had on my work.

My first PR job gave me an even deeper appreciation for how senior leaders can influence workplace well-being. Our CFO was a regular at the 6 a.m. boot camp classes, and other senior leaders—and those of us who aspired to be one—followed suit. But it wasn't just the boot camp. He also organized company teams for everything from 5Ks to 200-mile mountain relays. I joined them all.

It was in that job that I also began experimenting with walking meetings. I'd read that walking together not only releases endorphins and improves well-being but also fosters cooperation—people moving side by side in the same direction are more aligned in achieving shared goals.

At Target, I carried this practice forward, holding 1:1 meetings as walking conversations—either outdoors or in Minneapolis' extensive indoor skyway system, depending on the weather. The company also made well-being a priority by investing in incredible facilities, including indoor secure parking for bikes, showers, locker rooms, and even bike maintenance classes, tools, and supplies.

At Progressive, every building had an on-site fitness center, and just across the street, a beautiful, wooded park along a river with miles of trails provided the perfect setting for outdoor meetings. The company's long, low buildings, filled with stunning modern art, lent themselves naturally to productive indoor walking conversations.

Early on, I led a team in organizing a city-wide scavenger hunt along the Lake Erie shoreline, connecting Cleveland's cultural gems. The only way to move from one point to the next was on foot, by bike, or via public transit. The camaraderie built that day paid dividends for years.

I've never seen the need for well-being—both physical and emotional—be as acute as it was in early 2020 during my time at Nationwide. Taking remote meetings audio-only while walking outside in the sunshine proved to be a serious performance and mood booster. And as the pandemic stretched on, the team's need for healing extended beyond the physical. We created a safe space to share how we were feeling and to seek understanding. It didn't just help individuals—it brought the team together.

Now, as I write this in the spring of 2025, many companies are requiring a return to the office. Like all change, this will be difficult for many. As my friend and author, Jon Levy, says, the only thing we know for sure is that we'll get parts of this transition wrong.

As you approach this as a leader, I hope you'll consider some of the above ideas to help support your team's well-being and build camaraderie and collaboration. Just remember to put on your own oxygen mask before assisting those around you.

BRIAN GRACE

FOUNDER & PRINCIPAL, TRUE NORTH | FORMER CCO, NATIONWIDE

THE ART OF MEANINGFUL APPRECIATION: MOVING BEYOND "THANK YOU"

Picture this: A leader stands up at a town hall meeting and says, "I want to thank everyone for their hard work this quarter." While well-intentioned, this generic expression of gratitude often falls flat. Why? Because meaningful appreciation isn't about broad statements—it's about specific recognition that makes people feel truly seen and valued.

Three Keys to Meaningful Appreciation

1. Be Specific and Timely

Don't simply thank someone for "doing a great job." Instead, recognize the specific action and its impact: "Brian, your thoughtful questions during yesterday's client meeting helped us uncover a crucial insight that shaped our entire strategy. That kind of critical thinking is exactly what helps us win in the marketplace."

2. Match Recognition to the Person

Some team members thrive on public recognition, while others prefer a quiet word of thanks. Take time to understand how each person likes to receive appreciation. This personalization shows you care enough to acknowledge them in ways that resonate.

3. Connect to Purpose

Help people see how their contributions matter in the bigger picture. Instead of "Thanks for staying late to finish the report," try "Your dedication to getting this analysis right means our leadership team can make a more informed decision about expanding into new markets—a move that could create opportunities for our entire team."

Making It a Daily Practice

The most effective leaders weave appreciation into their daily routines. Here are three ways to start:

1. Begin Each Day with Intention:

Take two minutes each morning to identify one person whose contributions you want to recognize that day.

2. Create Appreciation Triggers:

After every meeting, ask yourself: "Who contributed something valuable that I should acknowledge?"

3. End Each Day with Reflection:

Before leaving work, send one specific note of thanks to someone who made a difference.

Common Pitfalls to Avoid

- **The Empty Thank You:** Saying thanks without being specific about what you're appreciating
- **The Delayed Recognition:** Waiting too long to acknowledge good work
- **The Unbalanced Approach:** Only showing appreciation to top performers or during major achievements

The Gratitude Multiplier Effect

When leaders consistently show authentic appreciation, it creates what I call the "Gratitude Multiplier Effect":

1. Recognition > Clarity:
People better understand what success looks like

2. Clarity > Confidence:
Teams become more willing to take smart risks

3. Confidence > Innovation:
New ideas emerge more frequently

4. Innovation > Results:
Business performance improves

5. Results > More Recognition:
The cycle continues and strengthens

Reflection Questions

1. When was the last time you received meaningful appreciation? What made it memorable?

2. Think about your team: Do you know how each person prefers to receive recognition?

3. What daily practices could you implement to make gratitude more consistent in your leadership?

REMEMBER:
Meaningful appreciation isn't about grand gestures—it's about consistent, authentic recognition that helps people feel valued and understood. When done well, it's one of the most powerful tools we have as leaders to build engaged, high-performing teams. And it doesn't cost a thing.

MAKING GRATITUDE WORK: A 90-DAY PLAN

Want a frame of a plan to integrate gratitude as a habit? Here's a structured approach to help:

First 30 Days: Lay the Foundation

- Audit your current recognition practices
- Map out key contribution moments that deserve recognition
- Create simple gratitude triggers in your calendar
- Start each team meeting by recognizing specific contributions

Days 31-60: Build the Habit

- Schedule weekly 1:1s focused purely on recognition and development
- Train other leaders on effective recognition practices
- Create channels for peer-to-peer appreciation
- Document the impact of recognized contributions

Days 61-90: Embed in Culture

- Link recognition to company values and objectives
- Share success stories across the organization
- Measure improvements in team metrics

Making It Real: Weekly Gratitude Practices

Choose one practice to implement each week:

- **Week 1:** End each day by sending one specific thank-you note
- **Week 2:** Start team meetings with recognition moments
- **Week 3:** Have gratitude conversations in 1:1s
- **Week 4:** Create space for team appreciation sharing

Leadership Action Guide

Ask yourself weekly questions:

1. What specific contributions have I recognized this week?

2. Where have I seen the impact of my appreciation?

3. What opportunities for recognition did I miss?

REMEMBER:
Gratitude isn't about being nice—it's about being effective. When we acknowledge contributions meaningfully, we create an environment where people naturally strive to do their best work.

THE DAILY PRACTICE OF GRATITUDE: MAKING APPRECIATION ROUTINE

As leaders, we often say we value gratitude but struggle to make it a consistent practice. Here's your practical guide to making gratitude as natural as checking your email.

Your First 10 Minutes

Start each day with these practices:

1. Gratitude Preview: Review your calendar for the day. Who will you interact with? What opportunities for recognition might arise?

2. Intention Setting: Choose one person you want to appreciate today. What specific contribution will you acknowledge?

3. Quick Connection: Send one brief message recognizing someone's recent work. Keep it specific and genuine.

Meeting Moments

Transform every meeting into an opportunity for meaningful recognition:

Before the Meeting

- Review the agenda for recognition opportunities
- Note recent attendee achievements
- Prepare examples of excellent work

During the Meeting

- Open with a specific appreciation moment
- Acknowledge real-time contributions
- Notice who helps move the discussion forward

After the Meeting

- Follow up with specific thank-you notes
- Document examples of great work for future recognition
- Share notable contributions with senior leaders

The Power Hour

Dedicate one hour each week (schedule it!) to these deeper gratitude practices:

15 Minutes: Recognition Review

- Review your team's recent work
- Note unrecognized contributions
- Identify quiet achievers

15 Minutes: Appreciation Planning

- Draft meaningful thank-you notes
- Plan recognition moments for upcoming meetings
- Schedule appreciation conversations

15 Minutes: Impact Documentation

- Record positive outcomes from recent recognition
- Note changes in performance
- Identify successful appreciation approaches

15 Minutes: Personal Reflection

- What recognition opportunities did you miss?
- Whose contributions need more attention?
- How can you make appreciation more meaningful?

Building Sustainable Habits

Use these triggers to make gratitude automatic:

After Every Meeting

- Who made a valuable contribution?
- What effort should be recognized?
- Who helped behind the scenes?

When Reviewing Work

- What excellence am I seeing?
- Who helped make this possible?
- What learning should be celebrated?

Before Ending Each Day

- What wins happened today?
- Who made a difference?
- What appreciation did I miss?

Making It Stick: The 21/90 Rule

First 21 Days

- Focus on one gratitude practice until it becomes automatic
- Set daily calendar reminders
- Track your consistency

Next 90 Days

- Add new gratitude practices gradually
- Document the impact you're seeing
- Adjust approach based on what works

Overcoming Common Barriers

"I don't have time."

- Start with 2 minutes each morning
- Use transition moments between meetings
- Combine gratitude with existing routines

"I might miss someone."

- Keep a running appreciation list
- Ask team leads for recognition suggestions
- Create systematic review points

"It feels forced."

- Start with what genuinely moves you
- Be specific about actual contributions
- Focus on impact, not effort

YOUR NEXT STEPS

1. Choose one practice to start tomorrow
2. Schedule your weekly Power Hour
3. Set up calendar triggers for regular recognition
4. Create a simple tracking system
5. Review and adjust after 21 days

REMEMBER: The goal isn't perfection—it's progress. Start small, be consistent, and watch how regular appreciation transforms your team's performance and engagement.

02

IN BUSINESS, SOMETIMES YOU JUST NEED TO LAUGH

Many years into my career as a strategic communications leader, I decided on a whim to try my hand at stand-up comedy in New York City. It was arguably the most nerve-racking day of my life. But I survived.

Just as I was breathing a sigh of relief and running for the exit after the show, the emcee approached me, describing my performance as "not half bad." That emcee was Clayton Fletcher, a successful New York comedian who invited me to perform with him the following weekend. I jumped at the chance to give it another shot, and a long-time partnership was born, one with a lasting impact on my career.

As I took to the stage more regularly with Clayton, I realized that my part-time stand-up experiences helped me better connect with clients in my public relations work. In general, I was becoming a better presenter. I was reading the audience better, picking up on verbal cues, and learning how to fill pregnant pauses with ease. Impressed, I hired Clayton to help train all of my employees at Peppercomm, a New York City-based communications firm that I had co-founded in 1995. To this day, Clayton still trains our employees to employ humor to improve communication skills and help show more vulnerability, empathy, and support to co-workers and clients.

I'm now a big believer in humor as a hidden secret sauce in the success of any business, so much so that in 2023, Clayton and I wrote *The ROI of LOL: How Laughter Breaks Down Walls, Drives Compelling Storytelling, and Creates a Healthy Workplace*.

For more than 15 years at Peppercomm, we've been cultivating a comedy-based culture that has helped transform us into a place where senior management is always open to poking fun at themselves in the name of laughter. I've seen firsthand how self-deprecating humor can quickly change the tenor of a room and begin to build trust. In many ways, humor is the entry point to breaking down walls, allowing leaders to demonstrate real empathy. And empathetic leadership is a game-changer for a stronger employee culture.

Recognizing that, I make it a point now to meet with every employee on a regular basis to understand what challenges employees face that I can empathize with, adjust workloads if necessary, and make it clear that I care. That habit is responsible, in part, for our amazingly low turnover rate. I know it's also why we've won one best workplace award after another.

That leads me to gratitude. Knowing how to loosen up and laugh has also helped me develop better relationships with my team. I do my best to over-communicate how grateful I am to our employees at every opportunity. When employees feel seen and recognized for how hard they're working and the many achievements they've scored, it pays huge dividends. In my honest opinion, it leads to a happier and healthier workplace. I also do my best to express gratitude to the many mentors for whom I've worked and without whose guidance I'd most likely be collecting tolls on the Garden State Parkway (not to denigrate toll booth collectors in any way, shape, or form).

Also in the spirit of giving back, Peppercomm hosts an annual fundraiser each January at the New York Comedy Club. Our employees select the charity, and I emcee (very poorly) for a group of performers that typically features Peppercommers, clients, media, guests, and the occasional street vendor. At that 90-minute event, we usually raise $5,000, which Peppercomm then matches. That event helps set a tone for a workplace culture that cares about its people and the community we serve.

I know that many of the best things about our culture come from celebrating laughter and taking ourselves less seriously. I may not have been "half bad" in taking on this comedy thing, but my team has been showing me up ever since, and our clients keep coming back for more.

STEVE CODY

SENIOR EXECUTIVE ADVISOR & FOUNDER, PEPPERCOMM

WELL-BEING AS A LEADERSHIP IMPERATIVE: A CONVERSATION ABOUT CREATING A THRIVING CULTURE

Another recent research study* we completed with The Harris Poll revealed a stark reality about workplace well-being that leaders can't afford to ignore. The numbers tell a compelling story: 76% of employees and 63% of managers feel burned out or ambivalent in their current positions. What's more, 89% of managers believe their employees are thriving, yet only 24% of employees agree. This perception gap is creating a critical blind spot for organizations, with constant change emerging as a primary driver of burnout.

Q: Why should senior leaders personally focus on employee well-being? Isn't that HR's job?

A: While human resources (HR) plays a crucial role, the research revealed something striking: Employees who thrive consistently point to one key factor—feeling supported by senior leadership. When leaders show genuine appreciation for their people and actively demonstrate care for their well-being, it creates a ripple effect throughout the organization.

Q: What's the connection between gratitude and well-being?

A: They're intimately linked. When leaders consistently show authentic appreciation, they create an environment where people feel safe and valued. Our research shows that thriving employees strongly agree with statements like "I feel proud of the work I'm doing" and "I feel respected at work." These feelings don't happen by accident—they're cultivated through regular, meaningful recognition from leaders.

Q: What actions can senior leaders take to promote well-being?

A: Start with these proven approaches:

1. Make well-being part of your regular conversation with your team. Don't delegate it or save it for annual reviews.

2. Share your own well-being journey. When you're open about taking time for exercise or mental health, it gives others permission to do the same.

3. Express appreciation for contributions that might otherwise go unnoticed.

4. Create space for real dialogue about workload and burnout.

Q: How can leaders balance the need for results with employee well-being?

A: This isn't an either/or proposition. Our research clearly shows that well-being and performance are deeply connected. When employees feel supported and appreciated, they're more engaged, more innovative, and more likely to go the extra mile.

The key is to make well-being part of your strategy for achieving results, not something that competes with it. For example, when you're setting ambitious goals, also discuss how you'll support the team in achieving them while maintaining a work-life balance.

Q: What's one thing leaders can do tomorrow to start making a difference?

A: Schedule individual check-ins with your direct reports focused solely on their well-being. Don't combine it with a regular status update. Ask questions like: "How are you really doing?" "What support do you need?" "What could we do differently to help you thrive?"

Most importantly, listen deeply to the answers and take action on what you hear. Remember, your genuine attention and appreciation are powerful tools for building the kind of culture where people can truly thrive.

Reflection Questions

1. When was the last time you had a conversation with your team that wasn't about tasks or metrics, but about their well-being?

2. How do you demonstrate that you value both results and well-being?

3. What's one well-being practice you could model for your team this week?

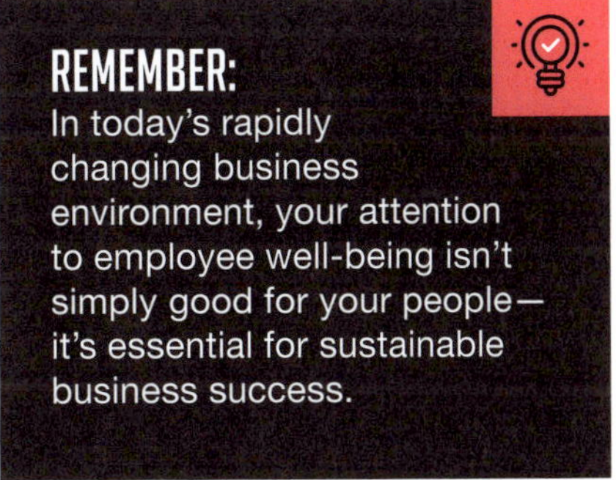

*The Grossman Group/The Harris Poll, "Burned Out & Checked Out: What Employees and Managers Need to Thrive," survey conducted online within the United States between January 11-16, 2024, and January 23-25, 2024, among 2,086 employed adults (aged 18 and over).

LEADERSHIP REQUIRES A COMMITMENT TO WELL-BEING

As the CEO of a top professional services firm in the US, I oversee hard-working, competitive professionals at the top of their game in their respective fields of audit and assurance, tax, advisory, and consulting services.

I've found over the years that some of these professionals have a hard time taking time off. And to be honest, I was similar as I grew in my career as an audit and consulting specialist working with our firm's health care clients. Yet, as I've grown in my career, I've developed a deep appreciation for the concept of well-being. I now work to embrace well-being both personally and as a leader trying to set the tone for my team. From a personal perspective, I believe that leaders cannot be exceptional if they do not take a break to recharge and decompress. Any leadership role can consume you fully if you let it, but at some point, there is a clear diminishing return.

If you want to be a great leader for the long-term, you must find some time to separate your personal self from the leadership self. Whether it's quiet time to reflect, meditation, exercise, or prayer, taking some time to "be off" will make you much more effective when you must "be on" later.

My personal approach is that I'm fanatical about running three or more miles per day, nearly every day. It doesn't matter if it's before work or after work (or sometimes even during the day when I have a free hour), but it's the best way for me to reset my mind.

Another benefit of embracing your personal well-being is that it can set a great example for your team. You cannot expect those you lead to find time to reset or decompress if you don't do it yourself.

As much as I can, I try to be a positive example. As leaders, you can do that through all the small and big actions you take daily that are visible to your teams.

For instance, I regularly reflect on whether I'm demonstrating a lifestyle approach that people want to emulate:

- **Do I appear overly stressed all the time?**
- **Does it seem like I'm always working?**
- **Is my personal fitness slipping?**
- **If you hear those you are leading say, "I'd never want to have that life," you should really consider how to reset that narrative. For instance, I don't want my high potential "NextGen" leaders to run away from our firm because they think it's healthier to do so!**

CONTINUED...

Another way to set the right tone as a leader is to listen more closely and empathize with your team. I was reminded of this recently when conducting a presentation on change management at a leadership retreat for my alma mater, Harding University.

The goal of the talk was to teach college seniors about a skill that is vital, but sometimes not top of mind—the ability to be "change agile." In that discussion, we talked about two key attributes that, as leaders, will make change easier for any team to embrace. One of these is a critical part of the planning stage of any change initiative, and that's listening closely to those closest to the action so you don't make a bad assumption about a change process.

So often, we as leaders stay too high-level with change, and we can miss some critical steps in the process that, if implemented, can make the change easier and more effective. We must have the humility to know we don't have all the answers and trust the feedback of those closer to the client or consumer, the factory floor, the patient, or the innovation process. These are the folks who can suggest meaningful adjustments to a change plan and make the process better by pointing out things that, as senior leaders, we didn't even consider. Might taking the time to ask these questions and tweak your plan slow you down right now? Yes, it probably will. Will it save time in the long run?

ABSOLUTELY!

Another point we discussed was the importance of being empathetic with those going through change, recognizing that not everyone processes change in the same way. Change champions who are great listeners and observe how people respond to change can bring far more people along than leaders who just assume everyone navigates change the same way they would.

Some people have a high capacity for change just in the way they are wired, while others do not. If those with a high capacity for change fail to empathize with those needing more support and coaxing through the process, there will be much less buy-in overall and, most likely, the change initiative will fail.

CONCLUSION

I've seen all of this play out in my efforts to bring teams together to achieve our strategic goals.

There's so much that's being asked of everyone today to reach critical business goals and to go above and beyond for clients and consumers. A commitment to well-being and treating team members with respect and care is one of the best ways to build trust.

The inevitable result? A highly aligned group of committed team members willing to pay it forward with exceptional results.

TOM W. WATSON

PARTNER & CHIEF EXECUTIVE OFFICER, FORVIS MAZARS

BUILDING A CULTURE OF TRUST, FLEXIBILITY, AND WELL-BEING

Reflecting on leadership styles is a valuable exercise. As I was reflecting on my own leadership style, I think a core part of my leadership approach is leading with gratitude—actively showing appreciation, acknowledging hard work, and recognizing the importance of physical and mental well-being.

I make a conscious effort to recognize and celebrate my team's hard work, both within the team and in front of the Institute for Public Relations (IPR) Trustees and other stakeholders. I also strive to make my praise specific and meaningful rather than performative. In turn, team members actively acknowledge and support one another, often sharing their own "kudos."

One way we foster this culture of recognition is through our "Roses and Thorns" exercise at the start of our weekly team calls, where we reflect on personal and professional highs and lows from the past week. This practice not only encourages appreciation but also strengthens our sense of connection and support. Leading with gratitude doesn't just mean that you acknowledge people's hard work, but you "reward" them by creating a culture that cares for them. I believe that workplace flexibility is one of the key drivers of success. Research supports this: people are happier, more engaged, and ultimately more productive when they have the autonomy to manage their day, balancing both work and personal commitments.

During COVID-19, IPR introduced monthly wellness credits to encourage the team to invest in their well-being—whether that means signing up for an exercise class or unwinding with a facial or massage. Nearly everyone takes advantage of these credits, and when someone doesn't, I remind them that this is important. As a fully virtual team, we spend much of the day at our computers, so stepping away and clearing our minds is essential for productivity and happiness. I make a point to model this behavior myself. As a tennis fanatic, I share on our Slack channels when I'm heading to play tennis or attend a class. I also post when I'm going to a doctor's appointment or volunteering at my child's school. And in return, my team is comfortable sharing their updates, too. No matter what level you are at in an organization, taking care of your health, well-being, and family should not be an afterthought but a priority.

IPR closes our offices for two weeks over the December holidays, and we have Summer Fridays. These structured breaks recognize our team's dedication and hard work, especially during these quieter periods when we don't have major events. And through this culture, I would argue that our team is one of the most productive and committed out there. They passionately believe in the mission, show up every day, and bring their best. In return, I am here to support, mentor, and help them grow.

In addition to creating a culture focused on flexibility and well-being, I try to encourage a psychologically safe environment where employees can speak up, take risks, and know that mistakes aren't punished. If there is an issue, the team knows they can come to me right away so we can work together to find a solution. I always remain calm and model that behavior for employees. I also try to inject humor when appropriate. Plus, this helps employees remain calm. Leaders must be the flight attendants people look to during turbulence—steady, composed, and consistent.

When you have a strong, talented team, they become thought partners. I empower my team by asking, "What do you think we should do?" And when I make mistakes, I own them.

Ultimately, leadership isn't about power or control—it's about trust, respect, and shared purpose. And when a team feels valued, supported, and empowered, they don't just show up—they thrive.

A great leader doesn't just recognize this—they actively create an environment where people can do their best work and enjoy what they do.

BUILDING A GRATITUDE-DRIVEN ORGANIZATION:

A GUIDE FOR SENIOR LEADERSHIP TEAMS

As a senior leadership team, your collective approach to gratitude sets the tone for the entire organization. When gratitude becomes part of your team's operating system—rather than an individual practice—it creates a multiplier effect that transforms culture and accelerates results. Here are the key actions your leadership team can take to make gratitude a strategic advantage:

Align on Gratitude as a Business Strategy

Why This Matters: Senior teams that treat gratitude as a strategic imperative, rather than a "nice to have," see significantly higher levels of employee engagement and performance.

Leadership Team Actions:

- Include gratitude metrics in your organizational dashboard
- Tie into existing recognition platforms your company may host
- Make appreciation a standing agenda item in leadership meetings
- Share gratitude success stories in company communications
- Connect recognition directly to business outcomes
- Measure and track the impact of appreciation initiatives

2 Create Systematic Recognition Touchpoints

Why This Matters: When gratitude becomes systematic, it becomes sustainable. Build recognition into your existing business rhythms.

Leadership Team Actions:

- Start every executive meeting with specific appreciation moments
- Create monthly recognition roundtables
- Establish quarterly appreciation reviews
- Design annual gratitude celebrations
- Build recognition into your strategic planning process

3 Model Cross-Functional Appreciation

Why This Matters: Breaking down silos starts with leaders actively appreciating contributions across departmental lines.

Leadership Team Actions:

- Recognize contributions from other departments in team meetings
- Create cross-functional appreciation opportunities
- Share resources to support other teams' success
- Celebrate collaborative wins publicly
- Document and share cross-team success stories

CONTINUED

BUILDING A GRATITUDE-DRIVEN ORGANIZATION:

A GUIDE FOR SENIOR LEADERSHIP TEAMS

4 Develop Your Organization's Gratitude Capability

Why This Matters: Building a gratitude-driven culture requires developing appreciation skills at all levels.

Leadership Team Actions:

- Invest in gratitude training for all leaders
- Create recognition toolkits for managers
- Establish mentoring programs focused on appreciation
- Share best practices across divisions
- Measure and reward effective recognition practices

5 Build Recognition Into Your Talent Systems

Why This Matters: Embedding gratitude into your talent processes ensures it becomes part of how you operate, not just what you say.

Leadership Team Actions:

- Include appreciation skills in leadership competencies
- Evaluate recognition effectiveness in performance reviews
- Consider gratitude practices in promotion decisions
- Build recognition into onboarding programs
- Reward managers who excel at appreciation

6 Create Accountability for Gratitude

Why This Matters: What gets measured gets done. Create clear expectations and accountability for appreciation.

Leadership Team Actions:

- Set specific gratitude goals for each leader
- Track recognition patterns and frequency
- Measure the impact on employee engagement
- Include appreciation metrics in business reviews
- Share gratitude analytics across the organization

QUESTIONS FOR YOUR NEXT SENIOR TEAM MEETING

1. How effectively are we modeling gratitude as a leadership team?
2. Where are the gaps in our current recognition practices?
3. What systems could we create to make appreciation more consistent?
4. How are we measuring the impact of our gratitude practices?
5. What's one thing we could do differently starting tomorrow?

REMEMBER:
As a senior team, your collective commitment to gratitude sets the standard for your entire organization. When you move from individual appreciation to systematic recognition, you create the conditions for sustainable high performance.

2. LISTEN AND EMPATHIZE

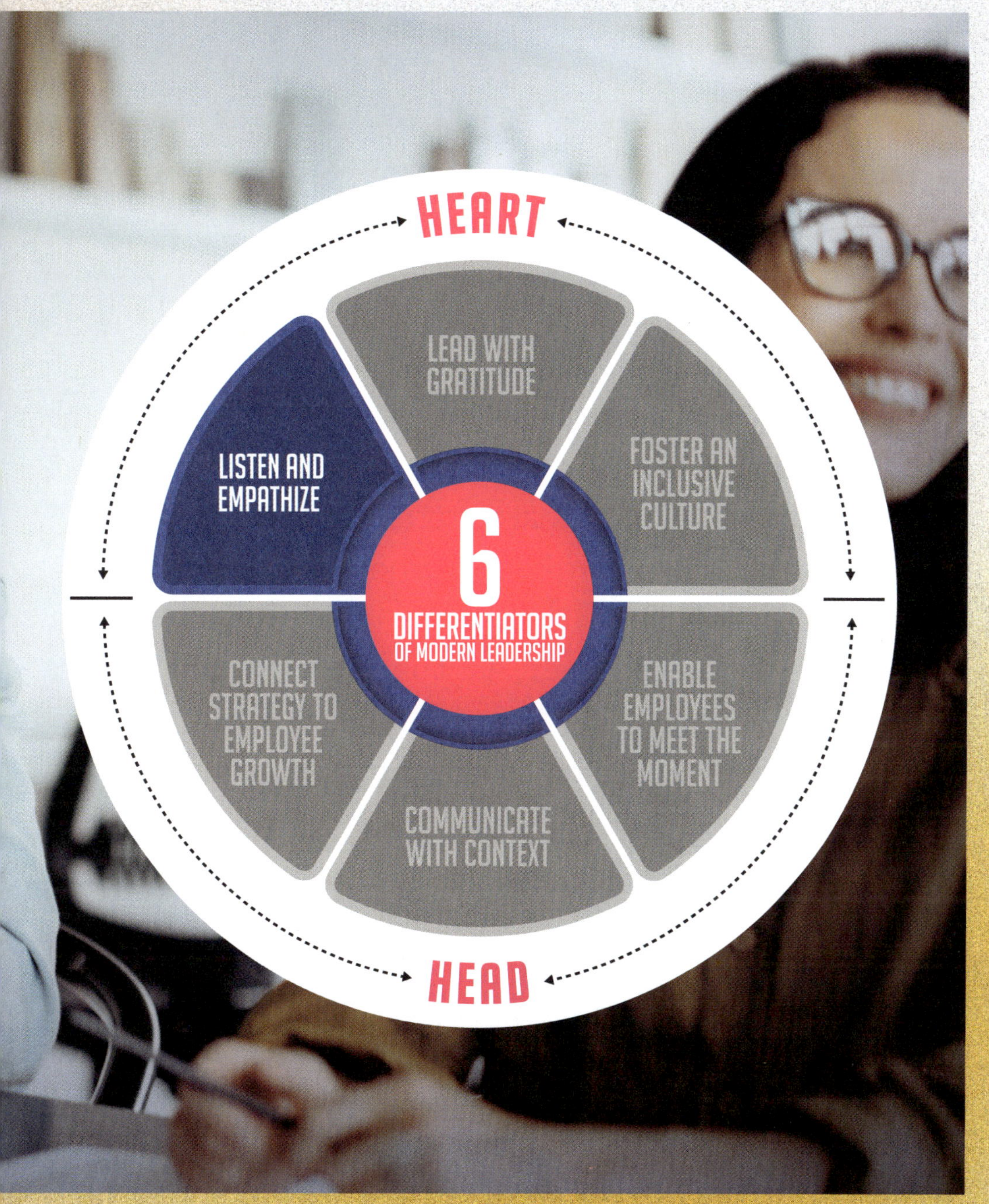
HEART
LEAD WITH GRATITUDE
LISTEN AND EMPATHIZE
FOSTER AN INCLUSIVE CULTURE
6
DIFFERENTIATORS
OF MODERN LEADERSHIP
CONNECT STRATEGY TO EMPLOYEE GROWTH
ENABLE EMPLOYEES TO MEET THE MOMENT
COMMUNICATE WITH CONTEXT
HEAD

In the complex landscape of Modern Leadership, two fundamental human skills have emerged as game-changers:

LISTENING AND EMPATHY.

These are not soft, peripheral abilities, but powerful strategic tools that can fundamentally reshape organizational culture, drive innovation, and deliver extraordinary business results.

Listening and empathy are deeply interconnected. Listening is the gateway to empathy—the ability to genuinely understand and share the feelings of another. It's not about hearing words, but about understanding the human experience behind those words. When leaders master this skill, they unlock unprecedented levels of team engagement, creativity, and performance.

Empathy is not about agreement or solving every problem. It's about creating a safe space where employees feel genuinely seen, heard, and valued. It requires vulnerability, curiosity, and a profound commitment to understanding others. Yet, listening and empathy don't come naturally to most leaders. They are skills that require intentional practice, ongoing development, and a willingness to challenge traditional leadership paradigms.

In this chapter, we'll deconstruct the art and science of empathetic listening. We'll explore why it matters, how to develop these critical skills, and the remarkable outcomes that emerge when leaders move beyond talking and directing and instead focus on understanding and connecting. Our journey will challenge you to reimagine leadership—not as a top-down directive, but as a deeply human practice of genuine connection, understanding, and mutual growth.

WHAT THE RESEARCH SAYS

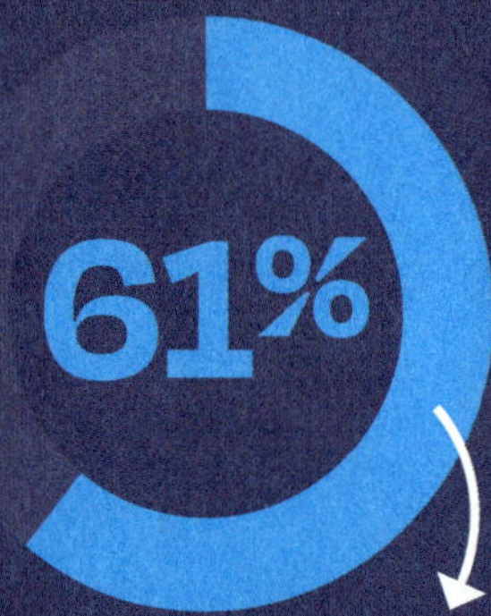

OF PEOPLE WITH HIGHLY EMPATHIC SENIOR LEADERS REPORT OFTEN OR ALWAYS BEING **innovative at work**

VS

ONLY 13%

OF PEOPLE WITH LESS EMPATHIC SENIOR LEADERS.[1]

SOURCE

[1]Van Bommel, T. (2021). The power of empathy in times of crisis and beyond. Catalyst.

Leaders who don't listen create a culture of organizational silence:

85% OF EMPLOYEES IN THE CORPORATE SECTOR HAVE REPORTED FEELING ***UNABLE*** TO RAISE AN IMPORTANT ISSUE TO THEIR SUPERVISOR.[2]

55%

OF CEOS THINK THEY LEAD WITH EMPATHY AT WORK, BUT

only 28%

OF EMPLOYEES AND ***22%*** OF HR SHARE THAT VIEW.[3]

[2]Dankoski, M. E., Bickel, J., & Gusic, M. E. (2014). Discussing the Undiscussable with the Powerful: Why and How Faculty Must Learn to Counteract Organizational Silence. Academic Medicine, 89(12), 1610-1613.

[3]Businessolver. (2024). 2024 State of Workplace Empathy: A Game Plan for Putting Empathy Into Action (Part 2). Businessolver.

THE POWER OF LISTENING BEFORE LEADING

I arrived with a notebook full of ideas for change when I stepped into a leadership role at an organization that had recently lost meaningful business and senior leaders. But sometimes the best leadership decision is choosing not to act—at least not right away.

During the interview process, I had formed strong opinions about what the team needed to be successful. The temptation to implement immediate changes was strong. However, I made a conscious choice to set aside my assumptions and instead embarked on a listening tour—scheduling 30-minute conversations with every single team member, which took months to complete.

I started with my direct reports to understand our culture and client landscape, then expanded these conversations across the organization. In each discussion, I asked five consistent questions:

- What inspired you to work here?
- Tell me about your current position and clients, and what you're most excited to be working on.
- What are you passionate about and/or would be your dream account or position?
- Are there any barriers holding you back from success?
- Is there anything else you think I should know?

What I discovered challenged my initial assumptions, reinforcing some and shifting others greatly. I found myself sitting across from a wide range of talented individuals with diverse backgrounds and deep passion for different aspects of culture. As a marketing leader, I immediately saw untapped potential—these varied interests and perspectives could create more innovative client work if we could better connect and collaborate.

But I also heard a recurring theme of isolation. Despite their individual talents, people felt siloed, working with just a few colleagues and unclear about our broader vision. They craved more opportunities to learn from each other and grow. This insight proved invaluable in reshaping our team structure successfully.

Making changes wasn't always easy. I had to advocate strongly for resources to strengthen internal communications and provide budgets for culture-building initiatives. But the results validated this approach. Within months, our team transformed from negative year-over-year growth to double-digit increases.

We began winning industry awards that had previously seemed out of reach, which in turn attracted new talent to our team.

The most rewarding outcome wasn't the metrics, though. It was seeing people thrive in roles that matched their passions, watching new collaborations form across former silos, and feeling the energy shift as people recognized their feedback in our new direction.

My key learning was this: resist the urge to validate your existing opinions. That's your ego talking. Stay open and flexible until you truly understand the situation from the ground up. The practical insights you gain from listening—really listening—to your team will lead to more sustainable solutions than any pre-conceived plan.

The satisfaction of seeing team members grow, tackle new challenges, and work on projects they're passionate about has been the most valuable experience of my career. It all started with the simple decision to listen first, act second.

SAMANTHA STARK

FOUNDER & CHIEF STRATEGIST, PHYUSION

EMPATHETIC LEADERSHIP— UNLOCKING GROWTH THROUGH LISTENING AND UNDERSTANDING

Leadership is often associated with strategy, vision, and execution; however, two of the most critical and overlooked traits of successful leaders are listening and empathy. These qualities are not merely soft skills; they are foundational elements that enable leaders to build trust, create meaningful connections, and drive cultural transformation within organizations.

When I stepped into the role of CEO at a well-established risk management and compliance technology company, I faced unique challenges. The executive team had been in place for decades, and many had far more experience than I did. Leading a digital and cultural transformation in this environment required more than just technical expertise or a strategic vision—it required a deep commitment to understanding my people.

In my first 30 days, I started conducting interviews with every employee in the company. The goal was not to dictate change but to listen and understand their perspectives, frustrations, and aspirations. What I learned from these conversations was invaluable: employees primarily wanted to feel heard and seen.

I was not offering immediate solutions or promising rapid changes. Instead, I created space for honest dialogue. By providing a platform for employees to express themselves without judgment, I gained deep insight into the underlying cultural challenges that needed to be addressed. These insights later formed the foundation for eight guiding principles that would reshape the company's culture and drive exponential growth. Over five years, these changes contributed to a 3x revenue increase—a testament to the power of listening and empathy.

Practical strategies for leaders:

1 CREATE A SAFE SPACE: Foster an environment where thoughts and ideas can be shared without fear.

2 PRACTICE ACTIVE LISTENING: Focus entirely on understanding without formulating a response or judgment.

3 SHOW EMPATHY: Recognize and validate different emotions and viewpoints.

4 EMBRACE DIFFERENT PERSPECTIVES: Seek to understand, even when there are differences in viewpoints.

5 ASK OPEN-ENDED QUESTIONS: Encourage deeper conversations by prompting others to share their thoughts fully.

6 REFLECT AND VALIDATE: Summarize key points to confirm understanding and show appreciation for the input.

Mastering these strategies is not just about improving communication; it is about shaping the culture of an organization. When leaders prioritize listening and empathy, they foster an environment where trust thrives, ideas flourish, and teams feel valued. This cultural shift is not merely a byproduct of good leadership; it is the foundation of sustainable growth and innovation. As a certified executive coach and CEO, I have worked with hundreds of executives across more than 10 nationalities, helping them integrate these principles into their leadership approach. Time and again, I have seen that the most impactful leaders are not just those with bold strategies but those who truly understand and empower those around them. By embracing listening and empathy, leaders do not just improve team dynamics; they transform the entire organization from within.

SAMUEL HON

CHIEF EXECUTIVE OFFICER, FIRST CORPORATE SOLUTIONS | ICF & BERKELEY CERTIFIED EXECUTIVE COACH

LISTENING PITFALLS: WHAT LEADERS GET WRONG

Leadership is a journey of continuous learning, and listening is perhaps the most challenging skill to master. Despite best intentions, many leaders unknowingly sabotage their own ability to genuinely hear their teams.

The Four Deadly Listening Sins

1. Listening to Respond, Not Understand

Most leaders are already composing their response before the speaker finishes their first sentence. This isn't listening—it's waiting for a pause to insert your own agenda.

Research from multiple communication experts shows that this approach:

- Blocks genuine understanding
- Makes employees feel devalued
- Creates communication barriers
- Reduces team psychological safety

2. The Expertise Trap

Many high-achieving leaders believe their success stems from having all the answers. Ironically, this mindset is their greatest listening limitation.

True listening requires vulnerability. It means:

- Admitting you don't know everything
- Being curious about different perspectives
- Valuing learning over being right

3. Emotional Filtering

Leaders often unconsciously filter feedback through their own emotional lens. A critique about a process becomes a personal attack. A suggestion feels like a challenge to authority.

This emotional defense mechanism:

- Prevents honest feedback
- Creates organizational blind spots
- Stifles innovation
- Erodes trust

4. The Interruption Syndrome

Watch most leadership meetings, and you'll see a familiar pattern: constant interruption. Leaders jump in, complete sentences, redirect conversations, and essentially communicate one message: "My time is more valuable than yours."

The cost? You're teaching others to be silent.

REAL-WORLD LISTENING FAILURE: A CAUTIONARY TALE

Kathryn, a senior vice president (VP) at a technology company, prided herself on being a "no-nonsense" leader. During team meetings, she would:

- Interrupt team members mid-sentence
- Provide immediate solutions
- Dismiss ideas that didn't immediately align with her vision

Her team's engagement scores plummeted and top talent began leaving. When an external consultant finally conducted exit interviews, the message was clear: Kathryn rarely listened effectively.

Breaking the Listening Barriers

Overcoming these pitfalls requires intentional practice:

1. Practice Radical Presence

- Put away devices during conversations
- Make eye contact
- Use non-verbal cues that show engagement

2. Master the Pause

- Count to three before responding
- Ask clarifying questions
- Resist the urge to problem-solve immediately

3. Embrace Uncomfortable Feedback

- Create psychological safety
- Thank people for their honest input
- Demonstrate that critical feedback is welcome

Reflection Questions

1. In your last three meetings, how many times did you interrupt someone?

2. When was the last time you changed your mind based on an employee's perspective?

3. Can you identify your primary listening barrier?

Your Listening Transformation Challenge

For the next week:

- Record your meetings (with permission)
- Review your speaking-to-listening ratio
- Ask a trusted colleague who can be a "truth-teller" for you for brutal honesty about your listening skills

The most profound leadership transformation begins with a simple, powerful commitment: to listen more, judge less, and create space for genuine dialogue.

07

LEAD WITH YOUR EARS, NOT JUST YOUR HEART

For years, leadership was often personified by individuals who could "command" a room with their oratory and executive presence. While those remain admirable qualities, leaders today need to bring their team members and external stakeholders along on the journey.

Doing so demands a deep understanding of human dynamics, a genuine connection with individuals, and the ability to foster trust and psychological safety. At the heart of this lies the power of **listening** and **empathy**. These two interconnected qualities are not just "soft skills" but essential components of effective, modern leadership.

Listening goes beyond simply hearing words. It involves actively engaging with the speaker, paying close attention to their verbal and nonverbal cues, and asking follow-up questions that elicit useful information. A leader who truly listens creates an environment where colleagues feel valued, respected, and heard. Listening is not just a skill. It's a mindset. And in an increasingly divisive and noisy world, active listening is both a lost art and a superpower.

Empathy is a natural companion to listening. Putting yourself "in someone else's shoes" allows leaders to see things from other perspectives and better understand their individual needs, motivations, and challenges. This doesn't mean agreeing with everyone or avoiding difficult conversations, but rather approaching them with understanding and thoughtfulness.

Listening and empathy are also essential for developing future leaders. By modeling these qualities, leaders enable team members to develop their own emotional intelligence and interpersonal skills, preparing them for leadership roles in the future. These qualities require conscious effort and practice, but they are indeed learnable skills.

Take me, for example. I am extroverted and enjoy telling a good story. I began my career as a lawyer, where I was trained to listen to respond—whether to opposing counsel, a witness, or a judge. I listened for weaknesses in reasoning, for openings to advocate. I listened to win.

Then I switched careers. Along my professional and leadership journey, I became more experienced with the profound difference of listening to understand vs. listening to respond or to solve. Two simple metaphors helped me immensely—the "spotlight" and the "iceberg."

Imagine keeping a spotlight on the person you're speaking with and try to avoid shifting that spotlight to yourself—even if well-intended to "relate." Instead, ask follow-up questions that keep the focus on the speaker. If you find yourself sharing a relevant story, keep it brief and return the focus or "spotlight" to the speaker with a question about their situation.

Applying the "iceberg" metaphor, listen for what's underneath the surface of what a speaker is saying, where values, needs, and motivations live. Listen, too, for emotionally charged words (e.g., "worried" or "thrilled") and seek to unpack those feelings—without assumptions or judgment—through open-ended and clarifying questions.

While I've come a long way, I'm still a work in progress. I still remind myself to put my phone away during conversations, so I am fully present. I still catch myself interrupting or quieting my inner voice that's begun formulating a response. By intentionally ingraining stronger listening habits into my daily life, however, I have become a more effective leader.

Likewise, I encourage rising leaders to practice quieting your inner monologue and truly hear the voices around you. You will be enriched by what you learn, by the connections you forge, and by the leader you become.

Because in the end, leadership isn't about having all the answers—it's about asking the right questions, and truly listening to the responses.

LARRY KRUTCHIK

EXECUTIVE VICE PRESIDENT, BURSON

THE POWER OF EMPATHY AND LISTENING IN COMMUNICATIONS

In communications, the ability to empathize and listen is not just an asset—it's a necessity. These skills elevate interactions from mere transactions to meaningful connections, fostering trust, understanding, and positive outcomes. Whether engaging with an audience, managing a team, or navigating a crisis, empathy and active listening are the cornerstones of effective communication.

EMPATHY: THE HEART OF CONNECTION

Empathy allows us to see the world through someone else's eyes, to feel their emotions, and understand their perspective. For communications professionals, this goes beyond delivering a message to deeply connecting with the people receiving it. Empathy enables communicators to anticipate needs, address concerns, and build genuine relationships.

Consider a corporate leader addressing employees during a significant organizational change. Without empathy, the focus might be solely on logistics or financial metrics, leaving employees feeling unheard or undervalued. With empathy, the leader acknowledges the anxiety and uncertainty employees may feel, offering reassurance and clarity. The result is a workforce that feels respected and supported, fostering loyalty and cooperation.

This principle was evident in 2016 when Conagra Brands moved its headquarters from Omaha, Nebraska, to Chicago—a monumental change for the company's employees and the Omaha community. Messaging during this transition was carefully tailored to address the concerns of both groups, and transparent, empathetic communication was key to maintaining trust. By acknowledging the impact on all stakeholders and demonstrating genuine care, Conagra preserved its Omaha legacy while successfully establishing a strong presence in Chicago.

LISTENING: THE KEY TO UNDERSTANDING

Empathy provides perspective, but listening brings clarity. True listening involves more than hearing words—it requires observing non-verbal cues, asking questions, and reflecting to ensure understanding. In communications, listening creates a two-way street where professionals gather insights while signaling that every voice matters.

At the onset of the COVID-19 pandemic, Conagra demonstrated the power of listening by distributing a survey to employees, seeking to understand their needs during that unprecedented time. Unsurprisingly, empathy and care emerged as top priorities. This feedback informed the company's actions, leading to the creation of the "Refuse to Lose" guest speaker series.

This virtual series featured experts in infectious diseases, mental health, and other critical areas, providing employees with answers, support, and connection during a challenging period. What began as a pandemic-era initiative has since evolved into a cornerstone of Conagra's internal communications strategy. Today, the series has welcomed cultural icons, chefs, philanthropists, civil rights activists, and more to share their stories and foster a culture of engagement and inspiration across the company.

CONTINUED...

08

EMPATHY AND LISTENING AS COMPETITIVE ADVANTAGES

In an era dominated by technology and automation, empathy and listening have become rare—and therefore invaluable—skills. Data and algorithms may drive efficiency, but they cannot replace the human touch. These skills allow professionals to interpret data meaningfully, craft resonant messages, and make decisions that prioritize people.

"BUILDING EMPATHY INVOLVES INTENTIONALITY: SEEKING OUT DIVERSE PERSPECTIVES, IMMERSING ONESELF IN OTHERS' EXPERIENCES, AND PRACTICING GENUINE CURIOSITY. SIMILARLY, LISTENING REQUIRES MINDFULNESS, PATIENCE, AND THE ABILITY TO SET ASIDE DISTRACTIONS AND ASSUMPTIONS. TOGETHER, THEY FORM A FOUNDATION FOR AUTHENTIC AND IMPACTFUL COMMUNICATION."

One strong example of the value of these skills is a professional network that I was privileged to help form during the COVID-19 pandemic. This group, comprising over 40 communications leaders from Fortune 500 companies, initially convened to discuss crisis management strategies surrounding the pandemic, including remote work, vaccine policies, civil unrest, and more.

Over time, it evolved into a supportive space where leaders could share challenges, seek advice, and collaborate. By fostering vulnerability and openness, this group has become a model for empathetic and effective professional dialogue.

CONCLUSION

Empathy and listening are more than tools—they are commitments to putting people first. They remind us that at its core, communication is about connection. For communications professionals, prioritizing these principles inspires trust, drives meaningful action, and creates lasting impact.

In a fast-changing world, where audiences are increasingly skeptical and authenticity is highly valued, empathy and listening are not just nice-to-have qualities—they are competitive advantages. By cultivating these skills, communicators can navigate complexity with confidence, forge deeper relationships, and ultimately, make a difference.

THE ANATOMY OF AUTHENTIC LISTENING: BEYOND HEARING WORDS

Authentic listening is an art form that transforms ordinary conversations into profound moments of human connection. It goes far beyond the simple act of hearing words—it's a holistic engagement that demands our full presence, emotional intelligence, and genuine curiosity.

At its core, authentic listening is a multidimensional experience that challenges everything we've been taught about communication. It's not about waiting for our turn to speak or formulating a response. Instead, it's about creating a sacred space of understanding where another person can fully express themselves.

Physical presence becomes the first gateway to authentic listening. This means more than simply being in the same room. It's about creating an environment of safety and openness. Put away the digital distractions. Make genuine eye contact. Lean in. Your body tells a story long before your words ever could.

Emotional intelligence emerges as the next critical dimension. True listening requires a deep self-awareness that allows us to recognize and validate others' emotional experiences. It demands that we suspend judgment, create psychological safety, and approach each conversation with radical curiosity. Dr. Daniel Goleman, a pioneer in emotional intelligence research, argues that this ability is the very foundation of effective leadership.

Cognitive engagement transforms listening from a passive act to an active process of discovery. The most powerful listeners approach every conversation as an opportunity to learn. They ask clarifying questions. They reflect back what they've heard. They challenge their own assumptions and remain open to entirely new perspectives.

Perhaps the most challenging aspect of authentic listening is **mastering the art of silence.** In a world of constant noise and immediate responses, sitting comfortably with quiet requires extraordinary discipline. Great listeners understand that silence is not empty—it's full of potential. It creates space for reflection, for deeper understanding, and for the speaker to fully express themselves.

The listening paradox is both simple and profound: The less you speak, the more impact you have. Authentic listeners don't solely hear words—they create the conditions for true understanding to emerge.

This journey of authentic listening begins with internal preparation. Clear your mind. Set an intention to understand, not to judge. Create psychological safety through a warm, open tone that communicates one fundamental message: You are welcome here.

As you develop this skill, remember that authentic listening is a practice, not a perfection. It's about being present, curious, and genuinely committed to understanding the human experience behind the words.

Reflection Questions

- When was the last time you truly listened without an agenda?
- What barriers prevent you from deeper listening?
- How might your relationships change if you approached every conversation with radical curiosity?

Your Listening Challenge: Embrace the 80/20 rule—listen 80% of the time, speak 20%. Keep a listening journal. Note the insights you gain when you open yourself to understanding. Reflect on how your conversations transform.

THE EMPATHY ROADMAP: A STEP-BY-STEP GUIDE FOR LEADERS

Empathy isn't a mystical skill reserved for a select few. It's a learnable, practical approach to human connection that can transform your leadership. This step-by-step guide will walk you through the art of genuine empathy, providing practical language and actionable strategies.

Step 1: Create Psychological Safety

Before you can empathize, you must create an environment where vulnerability is welcome.

What It Sounds Like: "I want to create a space where you can share openly and honestly. Whatever you're experiencing is valid." "I'm here to listen, not to judge." "This conversation is confidential and safe."

What to Avoid:

- Interrupting
- Offering immediate solutions
- Minimizing feelings
- Looking distracted or defensive

Step 2: Practice Active Listening

Listening is the foundation of empathy. This goes beyond hearing words—it's about understanding the entire emotional landscape.

What It Sounds Like: "Tell me more about what you're experiencing." "I want to make sure I understand completely. Can you help me see the full picture?" "What I'm hearing is…Is that correct?"

Techniques:

- Maintain eye contact
- Use open body language
- Nod to show you're engaged
- Reflect back what you've heard
- Ask clarifying questions

Step 3: Validate Emotions

Validation doesn't mean agreement. It means acknowledging the legitimacy of someone's emotional experience.

What It Sounds Like: "That sounds incredibly challenging." "It makes sense that you would feel frustrated given the circumstances." "Your feelings are completely understandable."

What to Avoid:

- "You shouldn't feel that way."
- "It's not a big deal."
- "Just get over it."
- Comparing their experience to others

Step 4: Ask Powerful, Open-Ended Questions

The right questions can create profound understanding and demonstrate genuine care.

Powerful Questions: "How is this situation affecting you?" "What does support look like for you right now?" "What do you need that would be most helpful?" "What's the most challenging part of this for you?"

Question Techniques:

- Use a gentle, curious tone
- Wait for a full response
- Show you're listening
- Follow up with deeper inquiries

Step 5: Recognize Non-Verbal Cues

Empathy extends beyond words. Learn to read body language, tone, and unspoken signals.

What to Notice:

- Crossed arms
- Avoiding eye contact
- Tone of voice
- Tension in body language
- Hesitation when speaking

What It Sounds Like: "I sense there's something more behind what you're saying." "You seem hesitant. Would you be comfortable sharing more?" "I noticed your body language changed. Is there something additional you'd like to share?"

Step 6: Be Vulnerable (Carefully)

Authentic empathy sometimes means sharing your own experiences, but with careful boundaries.

When to Share:

- When it genuinely connects to their experience
- To show you understand
- To reduce isolation
- Without making the conversation about you

What It Sounds Like: "I've faced similar challenges, and I understand how difficult this can be." "Your experience reminds me of a time when I felt overwhelmed." "I appreciate you sharing something so personal with me."

Step 7: Follow Through and Follow Up

Empathy isn't a one-time act. It's an ongoing commitment.

What It Sounds Like: "I want to check in and see how you're doing." "What support can I provide to help you through this?" "I haven't forgotten our conversation. How are you managing?"

Follow-Up Actions:

- Send a supportive message
- Offer specific help
- Check in periodically
- Remember details they've shared

Reflection Questions

1. Which of these empathy steps do you find most challenging?

2. Can you recall a recent conversation where you could have been more empathetic?

3. What emotional barriers might prevent you from fully connecting?

YOUR EMPATHY CHALLENGE

1. Choose one empathy technique to practice daily
2. Keep a journal of your conversations
3. Note the impact of your empathetic approach
4. Reflect on what you've learned

COMMON EMPATHY PITFALLS TO AVOID

1. Trying to "fix" everything
2. Comparing experiences
3. Offering unsolicited advice
4. Making the conversation about you
5. Rushing to a resolution

REMEMBER:
Empathy is a skill, not a destination.
It requires continuous practice, self-reflection, and genuine curiosity about the human experience. Modern Leadership happens in the moments of genuine connection—when someone feels seen, heard, and understood.

09

MODERN LEADERSHIP IS EMPATHETIC LEADERSHIP

In times of fear, uncertainty, and doubt, it is understandable to desire the protective armor of apathy. It might feel safer to run to the bunker of dissociation, disconnecting from our thoughts and feelings. But that's not what anyone would call leadership because leadership isn't about protecting yourself; it's about the courage to connect with others to create the conditions to achieve common goals.

Stephanie Mehta, the CEO and chief content officer of Mansueto Ventures, the media company that publishes *Fast Company* and *Inc.* magazines, recently identified the top traits for a CEO according to a recent survey. The results showed that humility, resilience, authenticity, and flexibility—characteristics that she says would have been unthinkable as a number one CEO trait in the 1990s—are the very skills that are needed today.

These so-called "soft skills" are increasingly recognized as crucial for leadership and decision-making. The World Economic Forum also stated in its most recent *Future of Jobs Report* published in 2023 that empathy and active listening, along with a host of skills like resilience, motivation, curiosity, and lifelong learning, were among the top 10 skills desired across all workforce levels. More and more, soft skills are being recognized as the new hard skills, or what I like to call "superior skills."

But what is the basis for these superior skills? I like to think that all roads lead back to empathy, the ability to understand others, see ourselves in a shared vision, and move in a collective direction. In today's volatile environment, the only way forward is together. We need empathetic leadership that is courageous enough to get uncomfortable at times. When things seem daunting, I recommend taking even the smallest steps to develop greater empathy.

Here are a few within reach:

1 COMMIT TO CULTURAL UNDERSTANDING. You don't have to travel to faraway lands to experience other cultures. Here's a pro tip: If your organization offers employee resource groups, consider joining a community different from how you identify. By definition, most ERGs are open to all and can serve as a gateway to other cultures and experiences. At my organization, I'm a member of six network-wide ERGs. I always come away from gatherings enriched—strengthening my thinking, creativity, and understanding. Being in spaces where my experience is not centered helps me grow my cultural awareness.

2 DEVELOP A GROWTH MINDSET.

Remember, it's never too late to learn new things. And the more I learn, the more I realize I have so much to unlearn, relearn, and learn anew. While I love learning difficult concepts, I'm also challenged by simple things like how to sew a button on a shirt. Learning both hard and easy things keeps us humble and teaches us to appreciate the skills of others.

3 WIDEN YOUR APERTURE.

Just like diversifying your investments is a smart strategy, the same is true by broadening what you read, watch, and listen to, as well. Exposure to other cultures, geographies, and genres makes us more informed and open-minded. One of my favorite things to do during the pandemic was connect with virtual book club members. We discussed fascinating topics across time zones and geographies. It was a great experience to learn from other perspectives.

Finally, as you take small steps to build empathy, I encourage you to also flex your muscles to fear just a little less, getting more comfortable with vulnerability and opening up possibilities. I'm excited for the reimagined ways people are recognizing superior skills to achieve big goals. The way forward is together. The way forward is with empathetic leadership.

SOON MEE KIM

EXECUTIVE VICE PRESIDENT & CHIEF DIVERSITY, EQUITY & INCLUSION OFFICER, OMNICOM COMMUNICATIONS CONSULTANCY NETWORK

LISTEN BEFORE YOU LEAD

"THE WISE OLD OWL LIVED IN THE OAK; THE MORE HE SAW, THE LESS HE SPOKE; THE LESS HE SPOKE, THE MORE HE HEARD; WHY CAN'T I BE LIKE THAT OLD BIRD."

It's a children's rhyme, and one I came to hate at the ripe old age of nine. But I remember it still to this day for the important lesson it taught me. It's far better to listen than to speak.

You see, I was a talkative, gregarious child. Every six weeks, Mrs. Ferrell would fill out my progress report which had good grades and one consistent conduct comment: "Excessive talking."

One day in particular, she was done with me. Too much talking and disrupting others, and she decided to give me a "detention" of sorts. I had to write 500 times in a spiral notebook the lesson of the wise old owl. I cried, my hand cramped, and I never talked too much again. That lesson has served me well as a grown-up in business, too.

Sometimes, as leaders, we feel the pressure to know everything, fill the room with our voices to prove to others our worth, and have the answer to every question. But, often, that means we spend too much time talking and not enough time listening. There are so many times in business where, when we take the time to listen, the advice we give, the counsel we offer, or the discussion we have with a team member, is much better, on point, or more productive.

How many times have you realized you were so concerned with your response to something in a live conversation that you didn't actually listen to the discussion happening in the room? I can think of dozens of times, and that is why when I get up each day, my mantra in the mirror is "try and be a better listener today."

To be a better listener, there are a few simple things you can practice:

1 ASK clarifying questions to be sure you understand what the person is trying to convey.

2 PARAPHRASE or "parrot" back what you think you heard to be sure it's actually what the person meant.

3 SEEK first to understand, and you can only do that by listening; if you are overly concerned about what you are going to say next, then you are not listening.

4 DON'T BE A "TOPPER" when you say something like: "Well, you think that was hard, I remember when I…"—that will shut down a conversation, and it goes against all the guidance for setting up psychological safety.

I remember a discussion with a team member where I thought he was asking to be removed from a project. I assumed he was complaining about a co-worker, but luckily, I remembered to listen and ask questions. What was wrong with the project? Did I understand correctly that he wanted to leave the project team? Turns out he wasn't complaining about a co-worker, nor did he want to be taken off the team. He didn't think the task we gave him for project management was right; he thought a co-worker would be better suited for that task and he wanted to focus on operationalizing the findings. Ah-ha! I'm still a student of this skill; I'd love to say I'm an expert listener, but I'm still learning. I'm sure you've been "listening," but I know I'm a better leader for taking to heart the lesson from the wise old owl. That is, slow down and spend less time speaking and more time listening. Learning to listen before I lead has helped me get to know my teams and people, understand what motivates them, ask clarifying questions, and resist the temptation to "top," which will drown psychological safety.

LINDA RUTHERFORD

EXECUTIVE ADVISOR, SOUTHWEST AIRLINES COMPANY

THE POWER OF ACTIVE LISTENING & THOUGHTFULNESS IN LEADERSHIP

In today's interconnected world, we are working in teams that are more diverse than ever. Thanks to globalization, we are closer to people from all over the globe, exposing us to an incredible variety of cultures, experiences, and perspectives. I firmly believe that diversity is one of our greatest strengths, but I also understand that it can be challenging at times to fully understand and effectively collaborate with people whose backgrounds and experiences are different from our own. That's why I think active listening and thoughtfulness are two essential elements of strong leadership.

Active listening involves truly focusing on what others have to say, engaging in meaningful conversations, and showing genuine curiosity about their perspectives. When we are in conversations, we often find ourselves planning our response while the other person is still talking. Active listening challenges us to shift this mindset. Instead of simply waiting for our turn to speak, it's about asking thoughtful questions, taking notes, and considering how the insights we gain can shape the way we lead. By prioritizing active listening, we create an environment where people feel heard, seen, and appreciated.

As President of the Public Relations Student Society of America (PRSSA), active listening has been a huge part of my leadership style. Born and raised in Buenos Aires, Argentina, where I still live, I have the privilege of leading an organization with student members from diverse backgrounds and chapters spread across the American continent. This experience has taught me how crucial it is to take the time to understand where others are coming from.

For example, when I joined the PRSSA National Committee, I quickly learned the importance of understanding my team's academic calendars, religious and cultural observances, and US holidays. By actively listening to my team members, I learned when their exams took place, which holidays they celebrated, and how all of this impacted their schedules. I used that information to make real adjustments, such as adding US holidays and cultural observances to my calendar and being mindful of deadlines during exam seasons. These small yet intentional changes made our collaboration smoother and showed my team that I genuinely cared about their experiences and challenges.

Another great example is our work with our Latin American chapters. As a member of a Latin American chapter myself, I'm aware that many of our Latin American students don't speak English, or even if they do, they don't always feel as comfortable communicating in English as they do in Spanish. After engaging in meaningful conversations and actively listening to their perspectives, a few National Committee members and I have been leading initiatives to incorporate more communication in Spanish, such as podcasts, social media captions, and articles. This has helped make our content more accessible and inclusive, ensuring that all students feel represented and understood, strengthening our sense of belonging.

Thoughtfulness goes hand in hand with active listening. It's not enough to just hear what someone has to say. We must also think about how to apply what we've learned in a meaningful way. This approach builds trust within a team and helps create an environment where everyone feels empowered to be their authentic and best selves.

In a globalized world, where teams are becoming more diverse, active listening and thoughtfulness aren't optional; they are essential for effective leadership. These elements have shaped my leadership journey, guiding how I connect with and understand those around me. By leading with active listening and thoughtfulness, I'm able to build stronger connections and create spaces where all perspectives are valued.

MILAGROS ORCOYEN

IMMEDIATE PAST PRESIDENT, PUBLIC RELATIONS STUDENT SOCIETY OF AMERICA (PRSSA) | CEO & FOUNDER, ENTREPUENTES

EMPATHY AT THE HELM: A GUIDE FOR SENIOR LEADERSHIP TEAMS

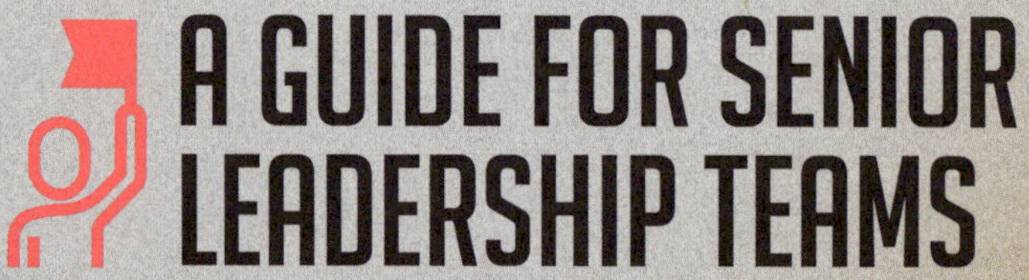

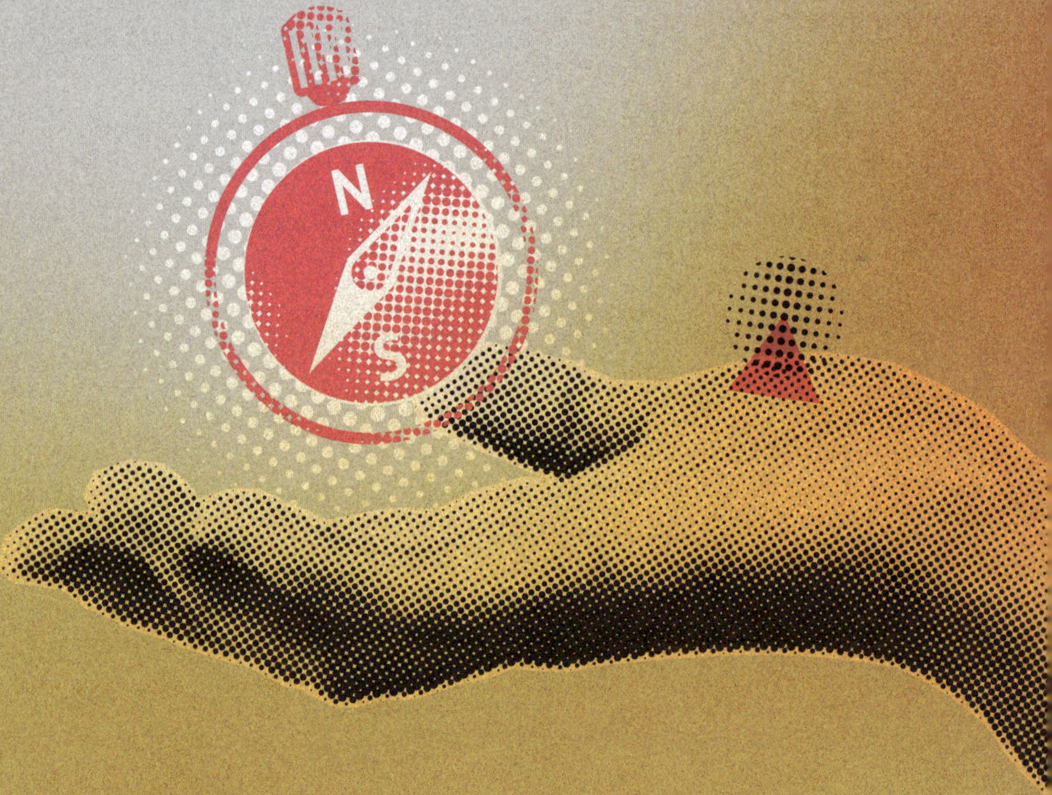

As a senior leadership team, your collective approach to listening and empathy sets the tone for the entire organization. When genuine understanding becomes part of your team's operating system—rather than solely individual intention—it creates a multiplier effect that transforms culture and accelerates human connection and performance. Here are the key actions your leadership team can take to make listening and empathy a strategic advantage:

1 Align on Listening and Empathy as a Business Strategy

Why This Matters: Senior teams that treat deep understanding as a strategic imperative and fundamental skill see significantly higher levels of employee engagement, innovation, and organizational resilience.

Leadership Team Actions:

- Include empathy metrics in your organizational dashboard
- Make active listening a standing agenda item in leadership meetings
- Share stories of breakthrough understanding in company communications
- Connect empathetic engagement directly to business outcomes
- Measure and track the impact of listening initiatives

2 Create Systematic Listening Touchpoints

Why This Matters: When deep listening becomes systematic, it becomes sustainable. Build meaningful dialogue into your existing business rhythms.

Leadership Team Actions:

- Start every executive meeting with dedicated listening moments
- Create monthly listening forums
- Design annual listening summits
- Build listening and deep understanding into your strategic planning process

3 Model Cross-Functional Empathetic Engagement

Why This Matters: Breaking down communication barriers starts with leaders actively seeking to understand contributions across departmental lines.

Leadership Team Actions:

- Practice active listening in cross-departmental meetings
- Create structured opportunities for deep, meaningful dialogue
- Allocate resources to support interdepartmental understanding
- Publicly celebrate moments of genuine connection
- Document and share stories of empathetic breakthroughs

CONTINUED

EMPATHY AT THE HELM:

A GUIDE FOR SENIOR LEADERSHIP TEAMS

4 Develop Your Organization's Listening Capability

Why This Matters: Building a culture of deep understanding requires developing advanced communication skills at all levels.

Leadership Team Actions:

- Invest in advanced listening and empathy training for all leaders
- Create communication toolkits for managers to lead by example and activate the culture
- Establish mentoring programs focused on emotional intelligence
- Share best practices for meaningful dialogue across divisions
- Measure and reward effective empathetic communication

5 Embed Listening into Talent Systems

Why This Matters: Integrating deep understanding into your talent processes ensures it becomes part of how you operate, not just what you say.

Leadership Team Actions:

- Include advanced listening skills in leadership competencies
- Evaluate empathetic engagement in performance reviews
- Consider communication depth in promotion decisions
- Build active listening training into onboarding programs
- Reward leaders who excel at genuine understanding

6 Create Accountability for Empathetic Engagement

Why This Matters: What gets measured gets done. Create clear expectations and accountability for deep, meaningful communication.

Leadership Team Actions:

- Set specific listening goals for each leader
- Track patterns of meaningful dialogue and understanding
- Measure the impact on employee engagement and organizational trust
- Include empathy metrics in business reviews
- Share listening analytics across the organization

QUESTIONS FOR YOUR NEXT SENIOR TEAM MEETING

1. How effectively are we modeling deep listening as a leadership team?
2. Where are the gaps in our current communication practices?
3. What systems could we create to make meaningful dialogue more consistent?
4. How are we measuring the impact of our listening initiatives?
5. What's one thing we could do differently starting tomorrow to enhance understanding?

REMEMBER:
As a senior team, your collective commitment to listening and empathy sets the standard for your entire organization. When you move from surface-level communication to systematic, deep understanding, you create the conditions for sustainable human-centric performance.

ACCESS POPULAR EMPATHY RESOURCES

FREE

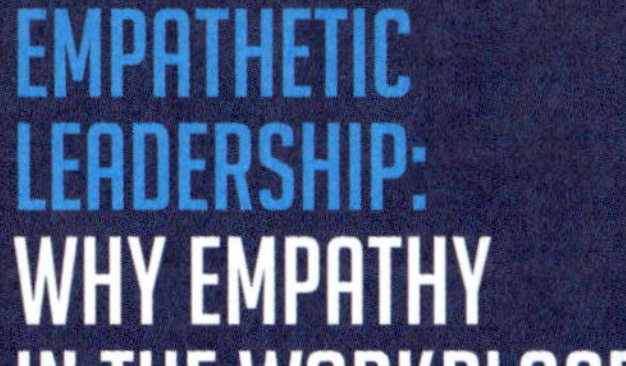

EMPATHETIC LEADERSHIP: WHY EMPATHY IN THE WORKPLACE MATTERS

Blog

LISTENING QUIZ

Tool

ACTIVE LISTENING: 8 STEPS TO BECOME A BETTER ACTIVE LISTENER

Blog

> "Empathy is about standing in someone else's shoes, feeling with their heart, and seeing with their eyes.
>
> - DANIEL H. PINK

3. FOSTER AN INCLUSIVE CULTURE

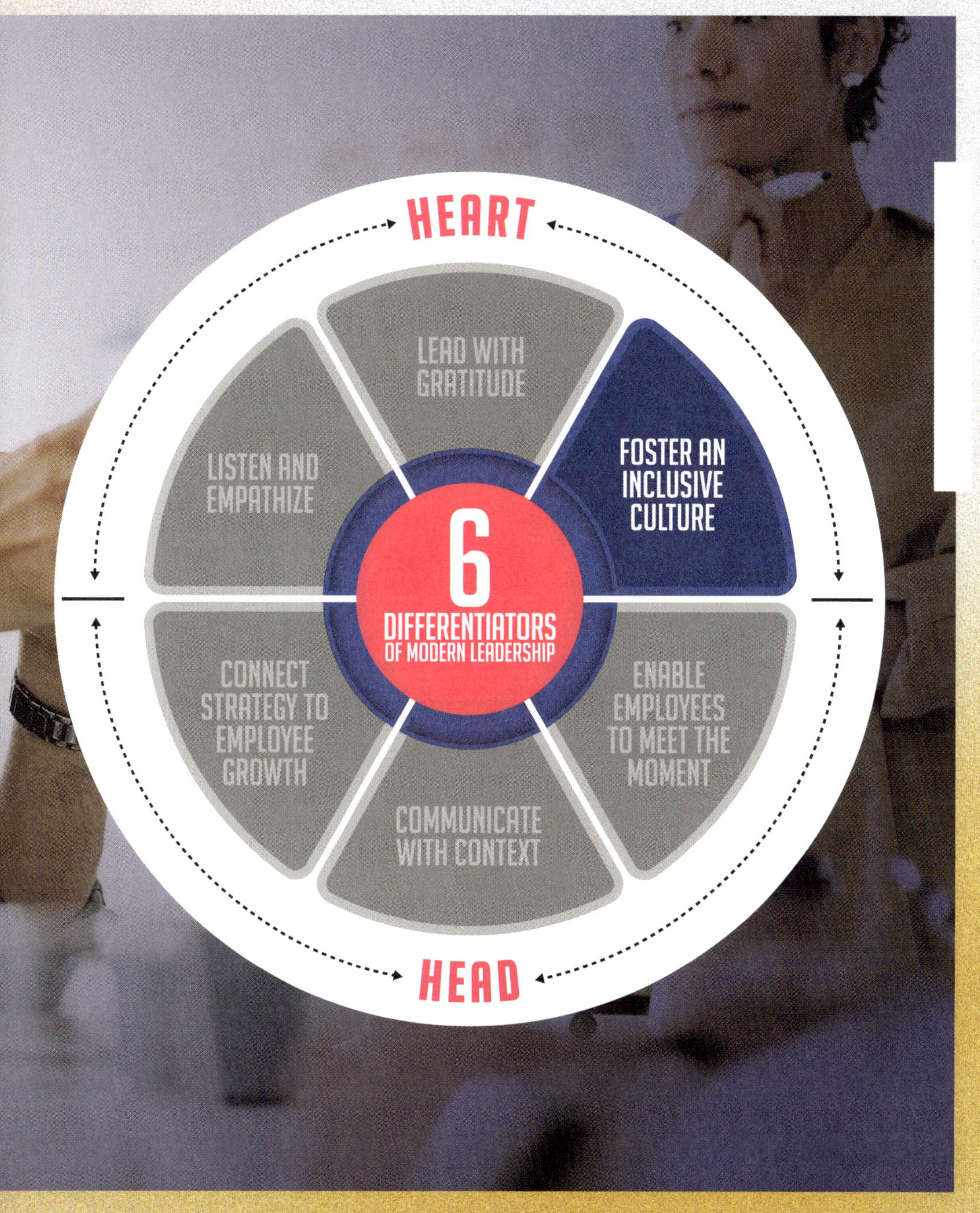
HEART
LEAD WITH GRATITUDE
FOSTER AN INCLUSIVE CULTURE
LISTEN AND EMPATHIZE
6
DIFFERENTIATORS
OF MODERN LEADERSHIP
CONNECT STRATEGY TO EMPLOYEE GROWTH
ENABLE EMPLOYEES TO MEET THE MOMENT
COMMUNICATE WITH CONTEXT
HEAD

WHEN IT COMES TO CULTURE, one truth stands clear: The most successful organizations are those where everyone knows "we're all in this together." It's not about having people in seats—it's about creating an environment where each person understands they're part of something bigger than themselves. Where teams support each other, celebrate collective wins, and face challenges as one united force.

Think about the last time you felt like you didn't belong somewhere. Maybe it was walking into a room where everyone seemed to know each other except you. Or perhaps it was joining a new team where everyone appeared to share an unspoken language of inside jokes and shortcuts. That feeling of being an outsider? It's more than uncomfortable—it's deeply demotivating. Now, imagine feeling that way every day at work.

The reality is, in many organizations, employees experience exactly that. They show up, do their jobs, but never quite feel like they're part of the team. But there's good news: Creating a culture where everyone feels they belong—where we're all in this together—isn't a nice-to-have; it's achievable. And it starts with leaders like you.

Throughout this chapter, we'll explore practical ways you can foster a culture where everyone feels seen, heard, and valued—where your entire team knows they're part of something bigger than themselves. You'll learn how to create an environment where team members don't survive but thrive together.

The journey to building an inclusive culture isn't about grand gestures—it's about consistent, intentional actions that show every team member they matter and that we succeed or fail as one team. It's about creating what I call "moments of belonging" that add up to a culture where everyone knows they're valued members of a unified whole.

When we embrace the mindset that we're all in this together, amazing things happen. Silos break down. Collaboration flourishes. Innovation soars. And most importantly, people show up excited to contribute to something bigger than themselves. Are you ready to build a culture where everyone belongs and where "we're all in this together" isn't a saying but a way of life? Let's get started.

WHAT THE RESEARCH SAYS

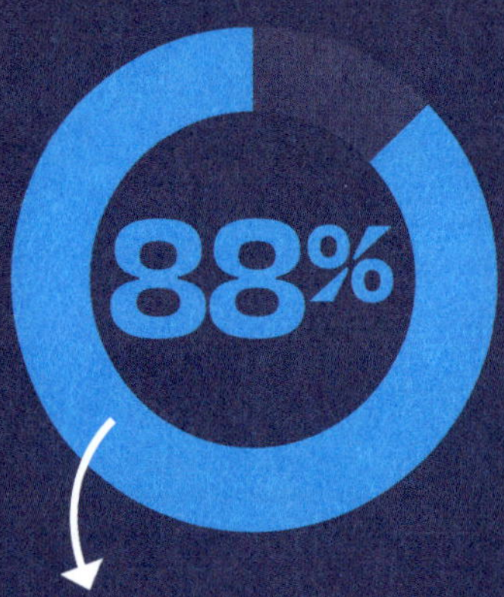

OF JOB SEEKERS CONSIDER A HEALTHY WORK CULTURE **vital for success.**[1]

Four of the top five REASONS EMPLOYEES LEAVE THEIR EMPLOYER GLOBALLY ARE TIED TO **workplace culture.**[2]

SOURCE

[1]Goodbread, J. (2023) Building A Company Culture To Drive Success. Forbes.

[2]Society for Human Resource Management. (November, 2023). SHRM Report Underscores Global Importance of Workplace Culture.

People are over 10 times more likely to quit

BECAUSE OF A BAD WORKPLACE CULTURE THAN BECAUSE OF THEIR SALARY.[3]

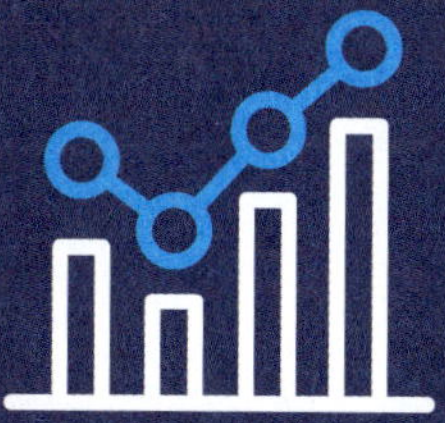

Belonging

WAS LINKED TO A

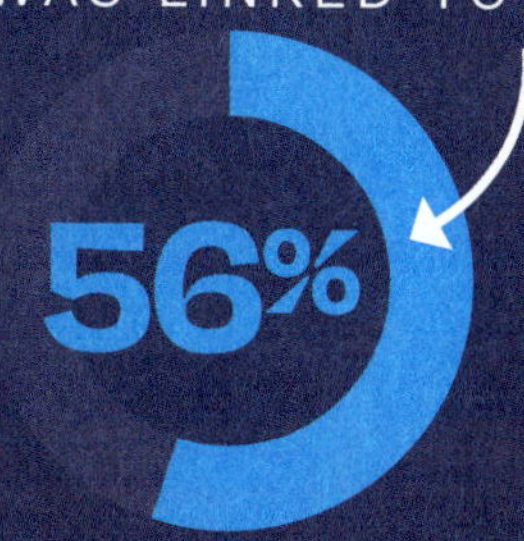

INCREASE IN JOB PERFORMANCE, A 50 PERCENT ***DROP IN TURNOVER RISK,*** AND A 75 PERCENT ***REDUCTION IN SICK DAYS***.[4]

[3]Sull, D., Sull, C. & Zweig, B. (January 2022) Toxic Culture Is Driving the Great Resignation. MIT Sloan Management Review

[4]BetterUp. 2020. "The Value of Belonging at Work: New Frontiers for Inclusion in 2021 and Beyond." 2020.

12

THE HEART OF HILTON'S SUCCESS

Imagine if CNBC's big story one morning was about Hilton's skyrocketing "culture quant," a figure that denotes the value of a company's ways of working. Of course, in reality, it's never going to happen. Culture is notoriously difficult to define, and even harder to measure.

Yet, away from the flashing, scrolling graphics of TV, culture may just be the most valuable asset a company has. And it might be easier to determine than some people think. To make this point with Hilton as an example, the story begins in 2007.

Blackstone had just purchased the company for $26B. Hilton was known then to be slow-moving, complacent, and lacking coherent direction. CEO Chris Nassetta joined that year and said in an *Inc.* article that employees "really didn't know where we were going," reminding him of a rowing team with oars all going in different directions. To make matters worse, the company was saddled with debt exceeding $20B. It was also deeply vulnerable during the global economic crisis that hit in 2009, losing 70 percent of its value during this period. Within four years though, Blackstone's purchase would become the most profitable private equity deal in history and the best leveraged buyout ever, according to *Bloomberg*.

Many stats and metrics can help show what led to these phenomenal results. However, before delving into any of those numbers, Nassetta always credits Hilton's success first and foremost to motivating, informing, and inspiring team members.

"We built a plan around purpose, building a great culture, making people feel like they were part of something bigger than themselves," he told the *Financial Times.* Importantly, these weren't just abstract initiatives either.

Lots of companies make the mistake of thinking of culture as "light" compared to the CFO's "hard," more tangible reports. Often, they'll have some sort of culture plan, sometimes called an employee value proposition (EVP), but the details lack substance, integration, and prioritization. In other words, they put up new posters in the break room, but none of it is ever fully absorbed into the employees' day-to-day.

On the other hand, Nassetta was a big fan of business guru Peter Drucker and would often mention his quote, "You can't manage what you can't measure." This point was essential to our culture plan, including evaluating the effectiveness of the extensive content that we pitched to the media, posted online, and featured on our intranet. We also surveyed team members often (e.g., after major meetings), monitored online sentiment (e.g., Glassdoor), conducted third-party research and focus groups, and targeted potential awards and rankings.

The most important designation to us was *Fortune's* 100 Best Companies to Work For, which provided a challenging "moonshot" goal since Hilton had never been chosen in the past. Ultimately, we not only made the list, but it didn't take long before we placed #1. Hilton also received several similar honors around the world, and we celebrated each of our big wins with great fanfare at our hotels and offices, which created more and more momentum.

Some other key elements from our culture plan were:

1 MAKE A STRONG IMPRESSION.

When revamping our Vision, Values, and Strategic Priorities at the start of Nassetta's tenure, we made sure they were memorable. The Vision came from a familiar quote from the company's founder, Conrad Hilton, "To fill the earth with the light and warmth of hospitality."

The six Values each began with a letter from the acronym HILTON (i.e., Hospitality, Integrity, Leadership, Teamwork, Innovation, and Now). The Strategic Priorities were simply worded, concise, and never changed year after year, which provided the framework for consistent external and internal communications, whether it be a quarterly earnings call or an all-hands team member meeting.

We benchmarked how much the Vision, Values, and Strategic Priorities were resonating across our 300,000 team members, including recall during our enterprise-wide annual survey. Within a few years of first launching them, nine out of ten team members around the world knew and understood them.

CONTINUED...

The Vision, Values, and Strategic Priorities were incorporated into the everyday jobs of our team members, including individual plans and performance reviews. Senior leaders were expected to walk the walk too, and those who weren't on board were exited out of the organization, particularly during a move of the company's headquarters from Beverly Hills, California, to Tysons, Virginia, which Nassetta credits as fundamental to the cultural reset. They were also now required to work various jobs at a hotel several days each year to connect to the business more.

2 PUT TEAM MEMBERS AT THE FOREFRONT.

Unfortunately, some companies launch a big campaign around their annual survey with phrases such as "we're listening to you," and then they ultimately don't. "Listening" is about more than just emailing the survey results. Companies need to empower managers to respond to feedback (what Nassetta called distributed leadership), and also report on progress throughout the year.

For example, a sore point for Hilton's team members for many years was that we didn't have a way to offer them discounted rates to stay at our hotels. So we launched a team member travel program, which became very popular and a great recruiting and retention tool. Even better, it actually made the company money because we were providing rooms that were heavily discounted but often would have otherwise gone vacant, so it was a win-win.

Right before our annual survey, we also reminded team members with infographic posters, emails, shift huddles, etc. of all the ways that we reward them and listen to their feedback. Some examples were parental leave, adoption benefits, and college assistance, just to name a few, and they all involved close collaboration with Communications and colleagues in other corporate functions, especially Human Resources, which was always an integral partner.

3 THINK BIG AND CREATIVELY.

Our culture plan's theme was "The Heart of Hilton," complete with a logo and branding guidelines. We sent a crew around the world to gather videos, photos, and testimonials of our team members across all our brands and major job functions. This content was used far and wide internally and externally, including our annual reports, corporate responsibility updates, and even our consumer-facing marketing.

We also launched a global Team Member Appreciation Week, which included visits by our leaders to share their thanks with food, DJs, and games. The Week's online toolkits for hotel general managers and HR directors included print-ready posters, tips on how to acknowledge team members, information on contests with multiple prizes, etc., and they were downloaded more than 5,000 times (exceeding the number of hotels we had in our entire global system).

Nassetta also knew that if our culture was to become more effective and enjoyable, he also had to lead by example and start from the top down. We began holding quarterly team member meetings, which were streamed globally from a different hotel each time, and they all had a very memorable opening.

Nassetta arrived on a horse in Dallas, danced with robots in Tokyo, rounded the bases with the mascots of the Nationals baseball team in Washington, D.C., and pretended to climb down the Burj Khalifa in Dubai.

During Nassetta's many visits to our hotels and offices, another sign of major progress also became evident. This one was more observational and qualitative, but still a very important indicator. When he first joined the company, the working environment was formal in many ways. Team members would sit quietly and unenergetically in meetings during presentations. Management would line up at attention in front of the hotel when his car would pull up, their postures as starched as their shirts. He was often referred to as "Mr. Nassetta."

However, over the months the culture began to shift, and team members would give him a warm handshake or hug when he arrived. Many would line up wanting to take a selfie with him. Others took him up on his offer to email him directly with thoughts and ideas. They got to know him as "Chris," who was a team member just like them—and who was dedicated to making the company very successful and the best possible place to work.

WHAT IS CULTURE ANYWAY?

I often ask leaders to describe their organization's culture. The responses typically start with phrases like "we're collaborative" or "we're innovative." But when I dig deeper with "how do you know that's your culture?"—that's when we get to what really matters.

Because culture isn't what we say we are—it's how we show up for each other every single day. It's whether people feel "we're all in this together."

Think about a great sports team you've watched or been part of. What makes them exceptional isn't individual talent—it's how they work together, support each other, celebrate victories, and bounce back from setbacks as one unit. That's culture in action.

The Four Truths About Culture

Through my work with organizations across industries, I've discovered four fundamental truths about culture:

1. Culture Lives in Daily Moments

It's not about mission statements on walls or values in handbooks. Culture lives in the small moments—how we respond when a teammate needs help, whether we make time to listen to each other, and how we handle disagreements. These moments tell the real story of whether we're simply in it for ourselves or in it together.

2. Everyone Shapes Culture, But Leaders Set the Tone

Your actions as a leader speak volumes. When you consistently show up as someone who puts the team first, who makes time to connect with people, and who celebrates collective wins, you're actively building a culture where people want to belong.

3. Strong Cultures Create Unbreakable Bonds

When people feel they're part of something bigger than themselves, magic happens. They look out for each other. They share ideas freely. They go the extra mile not because they have to, but because they want to support their team.

4. DNA That's Articulated and Lived Is What Great Cultures Need

While culture lives in moments, it must be guided by something bigger. Your vision, mission, and values aren't wall decorations—they're the foundation that guides every decision, interaction, and initiative. When clearly defined and consistently reinforced, they become the shared language that unites your team and shows everyone who we are and "What's important around here."

The Culture Test

Want to know your real culture? Here's a simple test: Watch what happens when:

- Someone on the team is struggling
- A mistake is made
- A new idea is presented
- Someone needs help outside their job description

The responses to these moments reveal whether you have a "we're all in this together" culture or if it's simply words on a wall.

Real Culture in Action

One of my favorite examples comes from a manufacturing leader I worked with. Every morning, he'd start his day walking the plant floor, not to check on production numbers, but to check in with his people. He knew everyone's names, their families, their challenges, and their victories.

When I asked him why he invested so much time in these conversations, his answer was simple: "Because we care about one another here. And when you care, you show up for each other."

That's one example of what real culture looks like—not saying "we're in it together," but showing it through our actions every single day.

Reflection Questions

- What made you feel most connected to your team this past week?
- How do you show your team members that you have their backs?
- When was the last time your team celebrated a win together?
- What's one thing you could do tomorrow to strengthen the bonds within your team?

Why Culture and Strategy Go Hand-in-Hand

A CEO I worked with and his team had developed what seemed like the perfect strategic plan—a comprehensive market analysis, clear objectives, and detailed action steps. But, six months in, little progress was being made. "I don't get it," the CEO told me in not-so-many words. "The strategy is solid. Why isn't it working?"

The answer became clear when I spoke with his team. While the strategy looked great on paper, people weren't executing it because they didn't feel connected to it—or to each other. They were operating in silos, focused on individual goals rather than collective success. The one-company spirit was missing.

When Culture Eats Strategy for Breakfast

You've probably heard the famous Peter Drucker quote about culture eating strategy for breakfast. But here's what that really means: The best strategy in the world won't work if your people don't feel united in pursuing it.

Think about it like a rowing team. You can have the most sophisticated race plan (strategy), but if the rowers aren't in sync (culture), the boat won't move efficiently—or might even go in circles.

The Power of Alignment

When culture and strategy align, something magical happens. I saw this recently with a manufacturing company that needed to rapidly change their production process. Instead of announcing the change, leaders brought everyone together—from senior managers to line workers—to understand the challenge and co-create solutions.

The result? Not only did they successfully implement the change, but they also:

- Reduced implementation time by half
- Uncovered innovative solutions from front-line workers
- Strengthened relationships across departments
- Created a sense of shared ownership in the company's success

Making It Real: The Three Keys to Alignment

Here's how to ensure your culture and strategy work together:

1. Make Strategy a Team Sport

- Involve people at all levels in strategy discussions
- Create forums where teams can contribute ideas and feedback
- Celebrate collective progress, not solely individual achievements

2. Connect the Dots

- Help everyone understand how their work contributes to the bigger picture
- Share stories of cross-team collaboration and success
- Make strategy discussions part of regular team meetings

3. Walk the Talk

- Model the behaviors you want to see
- Recognize and reward collaboration over competition
- Make decisions that reinforce "we're all in this together"

Signs You're Getting It Right

You know your culture and strategy are aligned when:

- People naturally help colleagues in other departments
- Teams celebrate each other's successes
- Problems are seen as "our challenges" rather than "their issues"
- Innovation comes from unexpected places
- People at all levels can explain how their work connects to company goals

REMEMBER:

Strategy provides the "what" and "where," but culture determines the "how" and "why."

When you get both working together—when everyone feels they're part of something bigger than themselves—that's when extraordinary results happen.

A Practical Exercise: The Culture-Strategy Check

Take 15 minutes with your team to answer these questions:

- How does our culture help or hinder our strategy?
- What behaviors do we need to encourage to achieve our goals?
- Where do we see people working together across boundaries?
- What gets in the way of collaboration?
- How can we better support each other in achieving our goals?

LET THEM EAT (KING) CAKE

When you're born and raised in the New Orleans area like me, good food and community go hand in hand. We not only look forward to our next great meal, but who we are going to invite to share that meal with, and the conversations and bonds we build over celebrating the food.

A wonderful way for teams to help foster an inclusive culture is to share food together, particularly those dishes that carry special meaning. For me, one of those special treats is a king cake. This colorful cake, which is steeped in hundreds of years of southern Louisiana tradition, celebrates Mardi Gras season, the period from Three Kings Day until Mardi Gras, the day before Ash Wednesday. These days many NOLA bakeries ship their king cakes around the country.

For the last fifteen years, I have held king cake parties with my classes and celebrated this annual tradition with my students. This memory sticks.

Years later students come up to me and call me the "king cake professor." Even better, students open up and share related traditions from their own families with the class. Over the years, we have talked about Rosca De Reyes, or three kings bread, which is celebrated around this same time of year in Latin cultures, and Paczki, the Polish donuts that are traditionally eaten on Fat Tuesday.

Students from Wisconsin have even talked about Kringle, the sweet, flaky, layered pastry with Northern European roots. I have done a variation of this "breaking bread together" when I do professional development workshops with groups and teams. Often, I will surprise the attendees with a more portable New Orleans treat, such as a wrapped pecan praline (Aunt Sally's is my favorite brand) or a mini Tabasco bottle.

This unexpected gift not only signals right off the bat to an audience that they're in for a good time, but that the person in front of them is open to sharing a part of themselves. Such unexpected personal gifts help us better understand the unique backgrounds and experiences of team members.

Sharing a meal together can even contribute to conflict resolution and (re)building trust. I often ask teams that are having issues working together if they've shared a meal or a drink lately—outside of the workplace.

When we share a meal or, in this case, a slice of king cake, we tend to let more of our whole selves shine through. We put down our guard and discover the commonalities we share as humans beyond the next work deadline. In a world where some forces are trying to sow division, fostering an inclusive culture has never been more important.

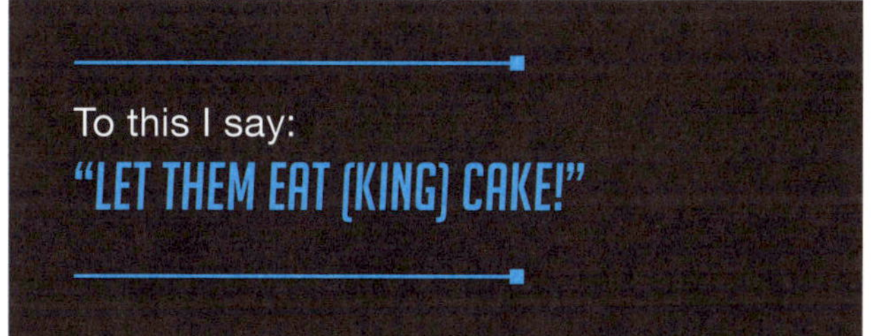

MATT RAGAS, PH.D.

PROFESSOR & DIRECTOR OF GRADUATE STUDIES FOR THE COLLEGE OF COMMUNICATION, DEPAUL UNIVERSITY | CO-AUTHOR OF SIX BOOKS, INCLUDING *BUSINESS ACUMEN FOR STRATEGIC COMMUNICATORS.*

14

ELEVATING ACCOUNTABILITY TO BUILD TRUST

As a business leader, can you identify the behavioral cause of the following four scenarios?

- You are the marketing director working against a sales report deadline. Your sales manager has repeatedly been asked for the data required to complete it. Their response has been "keep reminding me."
- A CEO mandates five days back in office while working from home three of those days.
- A team leader of a tech startup is openly critical of a team member, in the presence of their peers, for making a mistake.
- The executive team of a large health insurance company believes they are trustworthy based on their international expansion and increasing quarterly earnings, but their employee engagement is low, and customer turnover is high.

In 2018, Trust Across America assembled a committee comprised of members of our Trust Alliance, to identify universal trust principles, ultimately twelve, that could build trust in any team or organization of any size in any industry.

A year later we started a movement called TAP INTO TRUST, and today almost 200,000 people have accessed our principles at no cost: Truth, Accountability, Purpose, Integrity, Notice, Talent, Openness, Transparency, Respect, Understanding, Safety, and Tracking.

Precise descriptions can be found on our website (www.trustacrossamerica.com). We have since taken our work inside select organizations where proactive leaders acknowledge the costs associated with low trust and choose to address them before, not after a crisis.

As part of our program, we also offer a free online survey of interpersonal workplace trust, now completed by hundreds of individuals, to identify which of our twelve TAP behaviors people report as weakest in their own organization. The results have not wavered since we began tracking them in 2019: 42% report weak ACCOUNTABILITY.

The four opening scenarios are all examples of weak accountability at the individual, leadership, team, and organizational level.

LEVELS OF ACCOUNTABILITY

Our Trust Alliance has identified four levels of accountability and the actions required to elevate them.

1 PERSONAL ACCOUNTABILITY:

Behaviors starting with "self" and working outwards. A commitment to answer for and act on agreed-upon responsibilities.

Personal Commitments:

- I am intentionally choosing accountability
- I know what I am accountable for and who I am accountable to
- I take responsibility for my actions
- I take ownership when I make a mistake and do not assign blame
- I accept feedback
- My accountability includes holding others accountable

2 LEADERSHIP ACCOUNTABILITY:

Being responsible for upholding agreed-upon values and for delivering on team and organizational promises.

Leadership Commitments:

- I approach accountability from a positive, rather than punitive perspective
- I verbally clarify expectations
- When useful, I put expectations in writing
- I see projects through to the end and report on progress
- I always follow stated and understood values, not just when it's convenient
- I understand when it is appropriate to say "No"

CONTINUED...

3 TEAM ACCOUNTABILITY:

Holding one another accountable and taking responsibility without regard to level or role.

Team Commitments:

- We are all committed to our values and our projects
- Our intentions towards each other are always respectful and well-meaning
- We agree and abide by a set of team behaviors and accept the consequences when we do not
- If I am not accountable to my team, I expect others to let me know
- We follow up with facts and in a compassionate and empathetic way
- We know how to give and receive feedback
- When we fail at achieving a goal, we openly and candidly acknowledge it to our subordinates, peers, and/or supervisors
- We do not confuse accountability with responsibility

4 ORGANIZATIONAL ACCOUNTABILITY:

We deliver on all stakeholder promises.

Organizational Commitments:

- We execute and communicate to foster accountability
- We clearly communicate what we can and cannot do
- Management is accountable and accessible to all stakeholders
- We consider culture differences in accountability expectations
- All leaders are held to the same standards and demonstrate that no one is exempt from following our stated values

BUILDING ACCOUNTABILITY

Leaders cannot demand accountability without first modeling it, and this requires delivering on expectations and commitments. This is a simple plan to instill the importance of accountability in your team:

Role Identification: Team members understand their roles in elevating accountability.

Expectations & Goals: Identify them in a way that the team collectively accepts.

Do Not Be a Dictator: Work the accountability plan together. Get the early "buy-in."

Discuss It: Place the plan on the agenda for review, and make modifications with the team when needed. These are some discussion questions to bring to the team:

- Do we hold people accountable in a principle-centered rather than punitive way? If not, how do we change this?
- Do our accountability discussions demonstrate that we are on the same team? If not, how can we get them to show collective responsibility?
- When we fail at achieving a goal, how often and how do we openly, candidly acknowledge it to our subordinates, peers, and/or supervisors?
- How well do we hold all leaders to our standards and demonstrate that no one is exempt from following our stated values?
- What would such a system look like that honored this kind of accountability across all tiers within our organization?

No Excuses: Once the accountability plan is in place, enforce it as the leader and encourage it between team members. This means no excuses for missing deadlines, tardiness, too many mistakes, or low-quality output.

Recently, a friend relayed a story about a colleague who is **ALWAYS** ten minutes late for meetings. She said she "trusts" this person to always show up late. We laughed about the (mis)use of the word "trust."

But what my friend is actually doing is forgiving her colleague for her lack of accountability by ignoring her tardiness. My guess is she has never been spoken to about arriving on time.

While accountability is a large component of trust, it continues to be one of the most overlooked. Why not start the discussion today? And stop forgiving the tardiness.

BARBARA BROOKS KIMMEL

FOUNDER, TRUST ACROSS AMERICA-TRUST AROUND THE WORLD

CODIFYING YOUR CULTURE: WHEN IT'S TIME TO REFRESH, CREATE YOUR DNA TOGETHER

How do you know when it's time to refresh your DNA? Here are the clear signals that it's time to revisit your vision, mission, and values:

Your People Are Telling You

- Employees can't connect their daily work to the vision
- Your values feel like empty words on a wall
- People rarely reference the mission in decisions
- New employees don't resonate with the language
- Teams create their own interpretations

Your Business Has Evolved

- You've entered new markets or segments
- Your strategy has significantly shifted
- You've gone through a merger or acquisition
- New leadership brings different perspectives
- Your customer needs have changed dramatically

Your Culture Has Shifted

- The way work gets done has transformed
- Your workforce demographics have changed
- New generations bring different expectations
- Your industry faces new challenges
- The world around you has evolved

If you're seeing three or more of these signs, it's time to take action.

The Power of Co-Creation

Once you recognize the need for change, resist the temptation to gather your senior team in a room to rewrite everything. Or worse yet, have an individual draft the DNA. I've seen too many organizations make this mistake, emerging with perfectly crafted statements that fall flat because they don't reflect the voices of those who need to live them.

Here's a proven process for refreshing your DNA with your entire organization:

1. Launch Listening Tours

- Hold forums at every level of the organization
- Create safe spaces for honest feedback

- Ask what people love about your culture
- Understand what they wish was different
- Gather stories of your organization at its best

2. Form Cross-Level Working Teams

- Include voices from every part of the organization
- Mix generations and tenure levels
- Ensure representation from all locations
- Create roles for front-line employees
- Enable participation across time zones

3. Generate Initial Ideas

- Share themes from listening tours
- Workshop potential language together
- Test concepts with different groups
- Gather feedback on draft statements
- Refine based on input

4. Test and Validate

- Create feedback channels for all employees
- Hold working sessions to pressure-test concepts
- Ask people to share what resonates
- Look for disconnects or concerns
- Gather stories to bring words to life

5. Refine and Launch

- Incorporate the final round of feedback
- Share how input shaped the outcome
- Create tools for bringing words to life
- Train leaders on implementation
- Plan celebration and rollout

Making It Stick

The work isn't over when you unveil your refreshed DNA. Here's how to ensure it stays vibrant:

1. Connect to Daily Work

- Help teams link their work to the vision
- Share examples of values in action
- Create regular forums for discussion
- Recognize people living the values

2. Build in Regular Check-Ins

- Survey employees on connection quarterly
- Look for gaps between words and actions
- Monitor how vision guides decisions
- Gather ongoing feedback and stories

3. Keep the Dialogue Going

- Make vision and values part of regular meetings
- Create channels for continuous input
- Address disconnects openly
- Share success stories widely

Questions to Guide Your Journey

Before you begin, ask your team the following:

- How will we ensure every voice counts?
- What process will build the most ownership?
- How will we know if we've got it right?
- What systems will keep this alive?
- How will we measure impact?

REMEMBER:
Your DNA—your vision, mission, and values—aren't simply statements; they're the thread that connects everyone in your organization to a shared purpose. When people help create that thread, they're more likely to weave it into everything they do.

HOW TO IMPROVE YOUR CULTURE: MAKING "WE'RE ALL IN THIS TOGETHER" COME ALIVE

Recently, a senior leader asked me, "David, how do I actually improve our culture? Where do I start?" It's a great question, because while we all want a strong culture where everyone feels connected, getting there takes more than good intentions.

Let me share a playbook of sorts—practical steps you can take starting today to strengthen your team's sense of unity and shared purpose.

Start with Story Listening

One of the most powerful tools for building culture isn't talking—it's listening to others' stories. I learned this from a hospital CEO who transformed her organization's culture by starting every leadership meeting with one team member sharing their journey. "When we understand each other's stories," she told me, "we naturally start looking out for each other."

Here's how you can put story listening into practice:

- Set aside time in team meetings for people to share their experiences

- Ask questions about people's journeys, not solely their jobs
- Look for ways to connect different team members' experiences
- Share your own story in a way that invites others to open up

Create Moments of Connection

Culture isn't built in grand gestures—it's built in small moments that show we're in this together. Here are specific ways to create these moments:

1. Daily Check-Ins

- Start meetings by asking, "What do you need support with today?"
- Make time for brief one-on-one conversations
- Acknowledge personal milestones and challenges

2. Team Rituals

- Create regular celebrations of collective wins or progress
- Establish "help hours" where team members can seek support
- Start meetings with recognition of cross-team collaboration

3. Shared Experiences

- Create opportunities for teams to solve problems together
- Organize cross-functional projects
- Build in time for team members to teach each other new skills

Make It Safe to Speak Up

A culture of togetherness only works when people feel safe sharing their thoughts and concerns. Here's how to create that safety:

1. Model Vulnerability

- Share your own challenges and learnings
- Admit when you don't have all the answers
- Ask for help when you need it

2. Respond Productively to Problems

- Thank people for bringing issues forward
- Focus on solutions rather than blame
- Follow up to show you took concerns seriously

3. Encourage Different Perspectives

- Actively seek out different viewpoints
- Make space for quiet voices
- Acknowledge and build on others' ideas

Break Down Silos

Nothing kills a unified culture faster than departmental silos. Here are practical ways to break them down:

1. Create Cross-Functional Opportunities

- Rotate team members through different departments
- Form project teams with diverse representation
- Create mentor relationships across departments

2. Share Resources

- Encourage teams to help other departments during crunch times
- Create shared spaces for collaboration
- Recognize teams that support other departments

3. Celebrate Collective Wins

- Highlight how different teams contributed to success
- Share credit widely
- Create rewards that encourage collaboration

Make It Stick: The Follow-Through

Culture change only lasts when you build in ways to sustain it. Here's how:

1. Regular Check-Ins

- Survey team members about their sense of belonging
- Hold regular discussions about what's working and what isn't
- Look for signs that old habits are creeping back

2. Reinforce Through Recognition

- Celebrate behaviors that strengthen unity
- Tell stories of successful collaboration
- Create rewards that encourage teamwork

3. Adjust as You Go

- Ask for feedback on culture initiatives
- Be willing to modify approaches that aren't working
- Keep what works, change what doesn't

Quick Culture Check

Ask yourself these questions regularly:

- When was the last time I helped someone outside my immediate team?
- Do I know what challenges other departments are facing?
- Have I recognized someone for supporting their colleagues this week?

- What barriers to collaboration can I help remove?
- How am I showing my team we're all in this together?

REMEMBER:
Improving culture isn't a one-time event—it's a daily commitment to showing people they matter and that we succeed together. Start with one or two actions that feel most natural to you and build from there. The key is consistency and authenticity in whatever you choose to do.

MAKING SURE YOUR PEOPLE FEEL SEEN, HEARD, AND THAT THEY BELONG

It can be easy today to focus on metrics, deadlines, and deliverables. But there's something more fundamental that employees want, which drives performance: the basic human need to feel seen, heard, and to belong. When these needs are met, people bring their full selves to work. When they're not, even the most talented employees hold back, disengage, and eventually leave.

Here's how you can make these principles come alive every day:

Making People Feel Seen

- Learn and use people's names
- Notice when someone seems different than usual
- Acknowledge personal milestones
- Know everyone's superpowers and recognize their unique contributions
- Make eye contact in meetings, even virtual ones

Ensuring People Feel Heard

- Practice story listening, not just hearing words
- Ask follow-up questions that show you're engaged
- Act on input people provide
- Circle back to show others how their ideas made a difference
- Make space for quiet voices

Creating True Belonging

- Include people in decisions that affect their work
- Share the context behind changes
- Invite different perspectives
- Create opportunities for people to contribute their unique talents
- Make team success everyone's success

Creating True Belonging

- Include people in decisions that affect their work
- Share the context behind changes
- Invite different perspectives
- Create opportunities for people to contribute their unique talents
- Make team success everyone's success

Small Actions, Big Impact

The most powerful moments often come from simple actions:

- Starting meetings by checking in on people; don't dive right into work
- Taking a moment to thank someone specifically for their contribution
- Asking "What do you think?" and carefully listening to the answer
- Following up on personal details people have shared
- Making time for one-on-one conversations

REMEMBER:
People don't expect you to be perfect—they want to know they matter. Sometimes the smallest gesture, like remembering someone's child had a big game last weekend, can make the biggest difference.

CREATING MOMENTS OF BELONGING

Think about the last time you felt like you truly belonged somewhere. Perhaps it was in a meeting where your perspective wasn't just heard, but actually helped shape the final decision. These moments of belonging don't happen by accident—they're created through intentional leadership.

We often focus on the big initiatives to build inclusion, but I've found it's the small, everyday moments that make people feel they belong. These micro-interactions might seem insignificant in isolation, but they add up to create the connection that drives extraordinary performance. Here are five powerful ways to create moments of belonging:

1. Make Every Introduction Matter

When someone new joins your team, resist the urge to rush through introductions with a quick round of names. Instead, create space for people to share something meaningful about themselves. I recently watched a leader handle this brilliantly. Rather than the usual "tell us about your background," she asked each team member to share a moment when they felt most proud at work. The stories that emerged didn't just break the ice—they created instant connections and showed each person's values and motivations.

2. Turn Meetings into Connection Points

The first five minutes of any meeting are golden opportunities for building belonging. One technology leader I work with starts every Monday huddle by asking, "What's one 'Point of Progress' from last week you'd like to celebrate with the team?" Notice the framing—it's not about individual accomplishments, but about sharing success with colleagues. This simple practice has transformed his team's dynamics from competitive to collaborative.

3. Create "Visibility Moments"

Too often, the crucial work that keeps our organizations running happens behind the scenes. Make it a priority to spotlight these contributions. Recently, a health care executive made a point of visiting the night shift cleaning crew to understand their challenges. She then shared their stories and insights in the next leadership meeting. This wasn't solely about recognition—it was about making invisible work visible and showing that every role matters to the organization's success.

4. Build Bridges Through Questions

The questions we ask can either create walls or bridges. Instead of the standard, "How's that project going?" try questions that invite people to share their perspective: "What's something about this challenge that most people don't see?" or "How would you approach this if you had no constraints?" These questions don't gather information—they show people their insights are valued.

5. Honor the Whole Person

Belonging happens when people feel they can bring their full selves to work. A retail leader I know keeps a simple spreadsheet noting important events in his team members' lives—from children's graduations to elderly parents' health challenges. He doesn't do this to check a box. He does it because he genuinely cares, and it allows him to connect with his team as people, not employees.

Creating moments of belonging isn't about grand gestures. It's about consistent, authentic actions that show people they matter. When someone speaks up in a meeting, do you build on their idea and credit them? When a team member seems quiet, do you create space for them to contribute in ways that feel comfortable? These small moments add up to create a culture where everyone knows they belong.

The most powerful testament to strong moments of belonging isn't what people say in engagement surveys—it's what they do when times get tough. When people feel they belong, they don't survive challenges—they innovate, collaborate, and push through barriers together.

So tomorrow, ask yourself: What moment of belonging will I create today? Your answer to that question could transform someone's entire experience at work. And that's leadership that matters.

15

CREATE ENVIRONMENTS WHERE SENSITIVE TOPICS CAN BE OPENLY DISCUSSED IN A CORPORATE CONTEXT

You wouldn't think that in the twenty-first century, three companies that started in 1885, 1886, and 1917 would be teachers for creating places where sensitive, once unaddressed topics could be openly discussed. But Johnson Controls, Westinghouse, and Boeing became my incubators for creating these environments. In Spanish, we have a saying, "Paso corto, vista larga." Take small steps toward a big vision. As leaders, we have a vision, and getting the organization to come together to achieve it takes baby steps. For me, one of those small steps was creating a series of speakers who spoke openly about previously unspoken topics.

In 2020, my organization not only had to communicate about the pandemic, racial injustice in the US, and the need for belonging to something bigger while being isolated from one another, they also wanted to talk about these issues openly too. This is when the "Leadership Series" was born—a series of expert external speakers who spoke about belonging, the division between perspectives on race in corporate America, and mental health in the workplace, all subjects we had never heard discussed at work. It empowered employees, especially those of different backgrounds, to express their perspectives comfortably, something these old companies were not structured to do. The series was held during our weekly staff meetings. The interest became so great that our staff meetings doubled in size—standing room only.

Many of those who came were not in our organization, but they were welcomed anyway. When employees feel valued, appreciated, and heard, your vision is uncapped and the potential for baby steps to become even greater is enormous. While starting a company in the nineteenth century may have been simpler in terms of regulations, it was more challenging in terms of access to capital and allowing employees to speak openly on sensitive topics. They didn't see the need to.

Today, companies face more regulatory hurdles but have more access to global markets, and as important, leaders who understand their employees want so much more than a paycheck every two weeks.

> The progression of these very old companies teaches us that creating an environment for open discussion is not just possible but essential. By taking small, deliberate steps towards greater openness, leaders can bring out their organization's full potential. A workplace where employees are valued, heard, and not redirected.

16

SETTING YOUR TEAM UP FOR SUCCESS WITH RADICAL HOSPITALITY

ADAPTED FROM

Staying in the Game: Leading and Learning with Agility for a Dynamic Future

If you think about your first time coming into a new organization or team, starting a new job, or testing the waters of a new endeavor, you likely remember some accompanying anxiety. The bigger the stretch or further out of your comfort zone, the greater the potential unknowns and pitfalls that could come with it.

This was how I felt as I waited for Paul Seitz, the Membership Director for the Rocky Mountain Masters alpine ski racers, to pick me up in his mountain-weathered, green Ford Explorer that first day of training. My anxiety included the usual social jitters about whether I would be welcomed and taken seriously, along with the fear that I was completely delusional and getting in over my head. Having an ambassador, such as Paul, who met me at the door, ushered me in, introduced me around, and helped me understand "how we do things around here," as culture is sometimes described,[1] made the difference between these anxieties quickly dissipating or paralyzing me.

Senior leaders and their team members who embody agile leadership understand that no matter how much experience and expertise a new member brings to their organization, they will also bring some degree of social and logistical trepidation. These anxieties can be compounded if the new member happens to be "the only" of their demographic in the group, as I frequently am. Embodied Agile Leaders (EALs) are cultural ambassadors who don't just focus on improving their own performance; they help create the conditions for others to succeed.

When we arrived at our training venue that first day, Paul walked me to the clubhouse, made a round of introductions, and let me know when and where I should be ready to load the lift. These might seem like small gestures, but on the first day of any new endeavor, the basic logistics of when, where, and how can loom large.

Once our training group gathered at the top of the run that first day, everyone moved into action, helping set the course. Seeing that I wasn't sure how to contribute, Paul yelled out, "Pamela, shadow me!"

I skied down to where Paul was wrangling his share of gates to set when he promptly handed me a pair to insert into the holes the coach had drilled into the snow. As I followed his guidance, he leaned in and said,

"I WANT YOU TO DO THIS, NOT JUST SO YOU LEARN HOW THE DAY GOES, BUT SO EVERYONE ELSE SEES YOU HELPING. I WANT THEM TO SEE THAT YOU ARE ONE OF US."

Paul knew that if I was to feel included in this close-knit group of longtime members, I needed not just to show up but to become a contributing member from day one. He wasn't doing this just for me. Paul's 40 years leading international project teams at IBM taught him that groups can continue to thrive only if all members contribute to its success.

CONTINUED...

LEADING WITH RADICAL HOSPITALITY

My experience on the mountain that day and Paul's leadership have stayed with me years later. He didn't allow his years of experience to keep him from appreciating what it felt like to be a newcomer.

With agility, he shifted from his seasoned experience to the perspective of an anxious first-timer and, at every turn, helped set me up for success within an established culture. He was practicing something I have come to know as "radical hospitality."

I was first introduced to the term "radical hospitality" when interviewing an EAL whose playing field is the stage and screen rather than the mountain. Award-winning playwright and Tony-nominated actress and educator Anna Deavere Smith shared that radical hospitality, or the experience of being exuberantly welcomed and included, is needed if we are to bring our best performance.[2] Originating from the Rule of St. Benedict as an edict to welcome the stranger,[3] this practice seems especially radical and needed in polarized climates.

Affinity groups can play an important role in the workplace and other environments that want to foster an experience of belonging. The need for such radical hospitality initiatives heightens in spaces that have historically been dominated by one group, as is the case in many industries. Participating in activities and spaces where you don't see anyone who looks like you or shares your life experience (which is often true for people of color, LGBTQ+ people, people with disabilities, and others in predominantly White, straight, able-bodied arenas, such as skiing) amplifies the value of radical hospitality.

Being welcomed with radical hospitality by a leader with high emotional and cultural intelligence is uncommon for many, including me. Paul's leadership made such an impact on me because I realized that in all of my years working in various roles inside and outside of organizations, no one had ever taken this kind of care to welcome me and show others that I was "one of us."

The same is likely true for you. The good news is that each of us has the power to positively impact organizational culture by leading with radical hospitality and co-creating an environment where everyone can thrive.

PAMELA MEYER

LEADERSHIP AGILITY EXPERT & MASTERS SKI RACER

SOURCES

[1]Deal, Terrence E., and Allan A. Kennedy. Corporate Cultures: The Rites and Rituals of Corporate Life. Perseus Books, 1982.

[2]Butterworth, Scott. "Anna Deavere Smith to Deliver Scott and Fender Lecture," June 1, 2021. https://resources.depaul.edu/newsline/sections/debuzz/Pages/deavere-smith.aspx.

[3]Slocum, Robert B., and Victoria Slocum. "Radical Hospitality and Faith Inclusion: Lessons from St. Benedict." Journal of Disability and Religion, April 3, 2021. https://doi.org/10.1080/23312521.2020.1716917.

17

SILENCE IS NOT GOLDEN: THE VALUE OF CREATING A SPEAK-UP CULTURE

Most effective leaders have gotten the message about the importance of "listening" to your employees by now. ***(If not, you haven't been listening!)***

But what exactly have you been listening to? Do your employees feel safe to express themselves, even when their views don't align with yours? Or do they self-censor by withholding their ideas and opinions out of fear or disillusionment?

If the latter, then silence might not be golden at all. In fact, it might give you the false impression of workplace harmony. Harvard University Professor Amy Edmondson calls this phenomenon "the invisible silence," because employees withhold what they really think and feel. Instead, they tell you what they think you want to hear.

"No one gains from the silence," Edmondson explains in her book, *The Fearless Organization.* "Teams miss out on insights. Those who fail to speak up often report regret or pain. Problems go unreported, improvement opportunities are missed, and occasionally tragic failures occur that could have been avoided."

That's why creating an environment of psychological safety—one in which people can speak up without fear of embarrassment, rejection, or punishment—is so crucial to the success of high-performing teams and organizations. In fact, a two-year study conducted by Google known as Project Aristotle found that psychological safety was the most critical factor that distinguished its high-performing teams—even more than individual intelligence or technical skills.

Psychological safety is not about avoiding conflict. It's about creating a workplace in which all discussions—including disagreements—can be constructive, honest, and focused on solving problems rather than protecting egos. Team members can feel safe to take risks and express themselves in an authentic manner. While creating a genuine speak-up culture requires time and trust, here are four ways for you and your team to get started:

1. **CREATE** multiple channels for feedback, including anonymous platforms and structured small-group discussions. People express themselves most honestly when they can choose how to communicate.

2. **DEMONSTRATE** that speaking up matters by visibly implementing employee suggestions and publicly recognizing those who raise difficult topics.

3. **SHARE** concrete examples of how employee input has led to positive organizational changes. People need to see that their voice makes a difference.

4. **MODEL** vulnerability by openly sharing your own uncertainties and learnings. When leaders show it's okay not to have all the answers, others feel safer doing the same.

Effective leadership isn't just about finding the right answers, but also creating an environment where the right questions can be asked without fear.

FRANK J. OSWALD

FORMER LECTURER, COLUMBIA UNIVERSITY, M.S. DEGREE IN STRATEGIC COMMUNICATION PROGRAM

18

FOSTER AN INCLUSIVE CULTURE

We can all recall times when we've been in environments where we don't feel included or valued for who we are. This feeling usually makes us want to stay quiet and play it safe. Contrast this with times we feel so accepted that creative ideas flow freely from our minds into realized business results, and we are energized to perform, contribute, and take risks.

As a leader, one of my most important responsibilities is fostering an inclusive culture across my organization so that the best ideas are surfaced, the business achieves optimal results, and my team members are motivated, happy, and productive.

One of the ways I do this is by publicly celebrating employees who exhibit an open, fearless, and empowered attitude. Here's an example: When I joined Nokia nearly three years ago, I conducted skip-level meetings so I could hear firsthand from people throughout my organization. One such meeting was with a very junior team member working on social media. I asked for her feedback on how to improve my presence on LinkedIn. She assessed my profile and shared that I sounded too much like a corporate mouthpiece and recommended intermingling posts about company news with reflections on topics that are important to me as a leader. I loved her frank approach and realized she was spot on.

Soon afterward, I wrote a LinkedIn post about my favorite nonprofit organization and wound up with far higher levels of engagement than I do traditionally. Maintaining a strong profile on LinkedIn is important to me professionally because customers and partners who follow me can see important Nokia news supplemented by less expected content, and I was grateful for this employee's insight. In my next quarterly All-Hands call, I presented her with an award and showcased her as a role model of how I wanted people to challenge the status quo and speak their minds freely, including with senior leadership. Team members told me that this action made them feel that their ideas were welcome, regardless of their background or seniority.

I also foster inclusivity by celebrating diversity and supporting employee resource groups. For many years, I've mentored women and sponsored programs to develop female leaders. I was an executive sponsor for a Nokia women in leadership initiative that resulted in 22% of participants being promoted within two years. It was so rewarding to see these deserving leaders be recognized for their progress.

This year, I also became an executive sponsor for an LGBTQ+ program called OUTstanding leaders and worked closely with a team focused on Allyship training, which is designed to encourage employees to stand up for inclusion, equality, and equity. The team created an amazing video highlighting the benefits and easy steps to being an ally. Programs like this can help traditionally underrepresented groups feel included in the fabric of the company.

Finally, I focus on fostering inclusivity by structuring opportunities for my team members to develop new skills and participate in decision-making so they know their opinion matters. A recent example is a Shark Tank program I initiated, reserving a portion of our marketing budget for innovation and experimentation. Each quarter, I assemble a panel of individual contributors who serve as volunteer "sharks," listening to members of our leadership team pitch ideas to be funded. The sharks advise me on how to allocate the funding based on business impact.

This work also gives the volunteers a taste of the challenges associated with budget management and helps them feel included in decision-making while providing me with a broader set of perspectives. It's been a great experience and one we've all learned from.

I encourage all of us as leaders to remember the times we have felt that our voice doesn't matter and how that impacts our contribution. When we do everything in our power to turn that upside down, we can make important strides in creating a vocal, creative, and empowered workforce!

JEAN LAWRENCE

CHIEF MARKETING OFFICER FOR CLOUD & NETWORK SERVICES, NOKIA

BUILDING A "WE'RE ALL IN THIS TOGETHER" CULTURE:

A GUIDE FOR SENIOR LEADERSHIP TEAMS

As a senior leadership team, your collective approach ripples through every level of your organization. When employees see their senior leaders genuinely collaborating, breaking down silos, and supporting each other, it creates powerful momentum that energizes the entire organization.

Here are the key actions your leadership team can take to build a culture where everyone belongs:

1 Model Unity at the Top

Why This Matters: Senior teams that demonstrate unity in their actions, not solely their words, see significantly higher levels of collaboration and engagement throughout their organizations.

Leadership Team Actions:

- Start every executive meeting by recognizing cross-functional successes
- Make decisions as a unified team, not as individual functions
- Present organizational updates together, not in silos
- Show visible support for each other's initiatives
- Address conflicts openly and constructively as a team

2 Create Systematic Connection Points

Why This Matters: When connection becomes systematic, it becomes sustainable. Incorporate relationship-building into your existing business rhythms.

Leadership Team Actions:

- Hold regular cross-functional leadership forums
- Create monthly connection roundtables
- Establish quarterly culture reviews
- Design annual team-building experiences
- Make relationship-building part of your strategic planning process

3 Break Down Organizational Silos

Why This Matters: True unity starts with leaders actively bridging gaps between departments and teams.

Leadership Team Actions:

- Rotate leadership team members through different functions
- Create cross-functional project teams
- Share resources across departments
- Celebrate collaborative wins publicly
- Document and share cross-team success stories

CONTINUED

BUILDING A "WE'RE ALL IN THIS TOGETHER" CULTURE:

A GUIDE FOR SENIOR LEADERSHIP TEAMS

4 Develop Your Organization's Connection Capability

Why This Matters: Building a unified culture requires developing relationship skills at all levels.

Leadership Team Actions:

- Invest in team-building training for all leaders
- Create collaboration toolkits
- Establish mentoring programs across functions
- Share best practices for building unity
- Measure and reward effective team-building practices

5 Build Unity into Your People Systems

Why This Matters: Embedding connection into your talent processes ensures it becomes part of how you operate, not just what you say.

Leadership Team Actions:

- Include collaboration skills in leadership competencies
- Evaluate relationship-building in performance reviews
- Consider team-building success in promotion decisions
- Build connection into onboarding
- Reward leaders who excel at breaking down silos

6 Create Accountability for Unity

Why This Matters: What gets measured gets done. Create clear expectations and accountability for building connections.

Leadership Team Actions:

- Set specific unity goals for each leader
- Track collaboration patterns and frequency
- Measure the impact on employee engagement
- Include team-building metrics in business reviews
- Share connection analytics across the organization

QUESTIONS FOR YOUR NEXT SENIOR TEAM MEETING

1. How effectively are we modeling unity as a leadership team?
2. Where are the gaps in our current collaboration practices?
3. What systems could we create to make connection more consistent?
4. How are we measuring the impact of our unity initiatives?
5. What's one thing we could do differently starting tomorrow?

REMEMBER:
As a senior team, your collective commitment to unity sets the standard for your entire organization. When you move from individual leadership to systematic connection-building, you create the conditions for sustainable high performance.

ACCESS POPULAR CULTURE RESOURCES

FREE

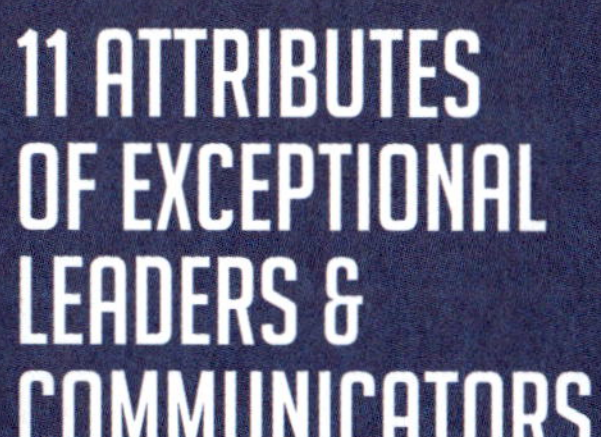

11 ATTRIBUTES OF EXCEPTIONAL LEADERS & COMMUNICATORS

eBook

HELPING PEOPLE GET TO KNOW YOU

Tool

STRATEGIC STORYTELLING

Tool

GUIDE TO ORGANIZATIONAL CULTURE CHANGE

Blog

4. COMMUNICATE WITH CONTEXT

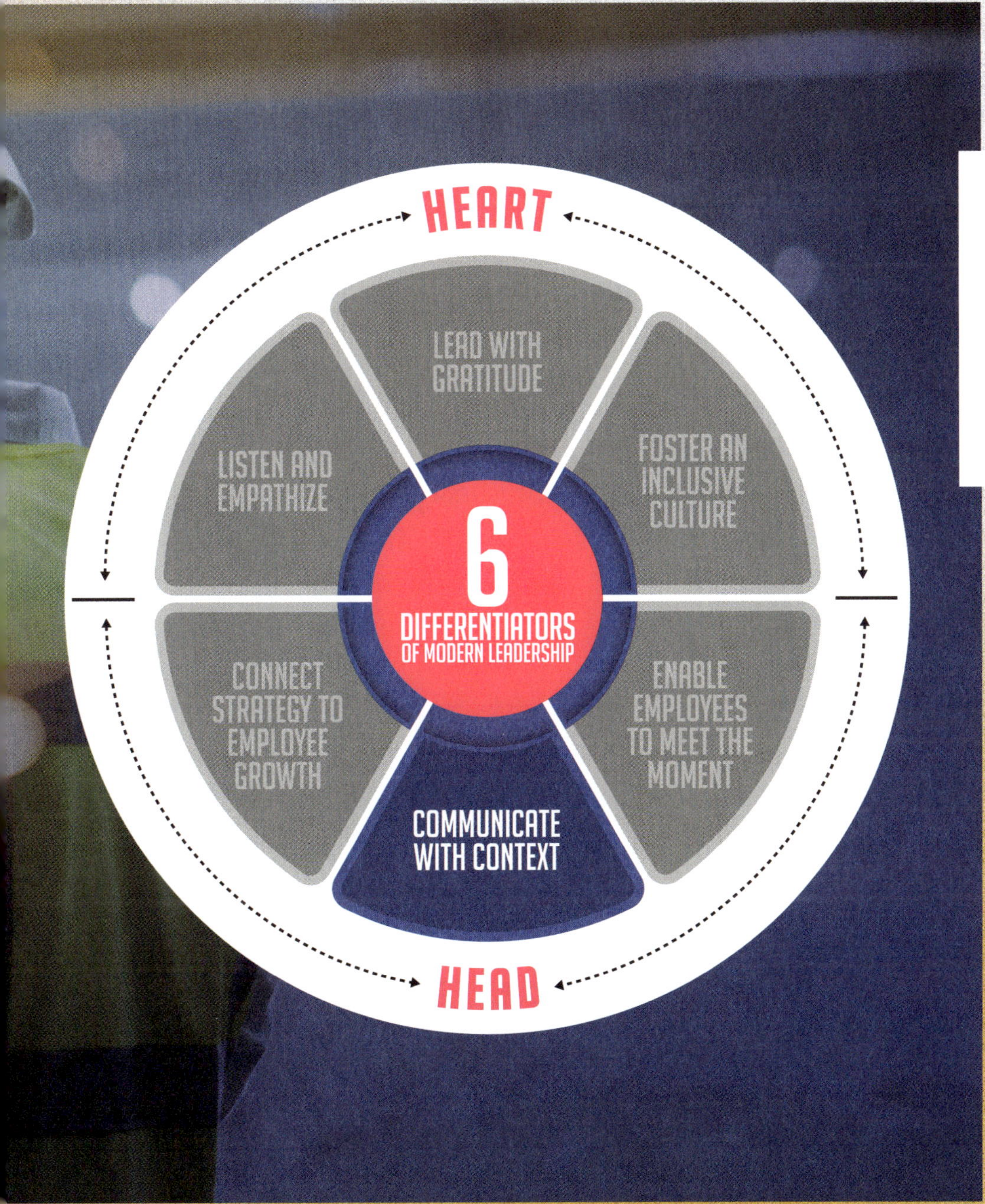

HEART

LEAD WITH GRATITUDE

FOSTER AN INCLUSIVE CULTURE

ENABLE EMPLOYEES TO MEET THE MOMENT

COMMUNICATE WITH CONTEXT

CONNECT STRATEGY TO EMPLOYEE GROWTH

LISTEN AND EMPATHIZE

6
DIFFERENTIATORS
OF MODERN LEADERSHIP

HEAD

Effective communication isn't just about what leaders say—it's about how well they connect their message to what matters most to their audience and move them to action. The most successful leaders understand a fundamental truth: Communication happens in the mind of the listener, not the speaker.

Leaders often focus on crafting the perfect message, choosing the right words, or mastering delivery techniques. While these elements matter, they often miss the most critical aspect of communication—

CONTEXT.

When leaders provide context, they help employees understand not solely what is happening, but why it matters to them personally and how it connects to the bigger picture. The best communicators consistently demonstrate an ability to frame messages in ways that resonate deeply with their audiences.

They recognize that employees are bombarded with information but starved for meaning. These exceptional leaders don't push out messages; they create understanding by providing essential context that helps employees connect the dots between organizational goals and their daily work.

In this chapter, we'll explore the key principles and practical approaches that enable leaders to communicate with context effectively. You'll learn specific strategies to build trust through transparency, shift from communicating from your perspective to your audience's viewpoint, frame messages to answer the fundamental question "What's in it for me?" and calibrate your communication approach based on what your audience needs.

Whether you're sharing major organizational changes or having routine team discussions, the insights and tools in this chapter will help you communicate in ways that connect with and motivate your people.

WHAT THE RESEARCH SAYS

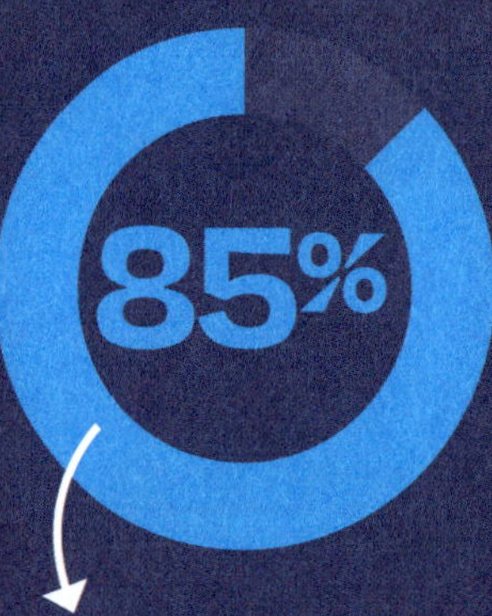

OF LEADERS THINK THE COMMUNICATIONS THEY SHARE HAVE THE CONTEXT EMPLOYEES NEED TO DO THEIR JOBS WELL—**ONLY 45% OF EMPLOYEES AGREE.**[1]

WHEN ASKED:

"How could your organization's leaders improve the essential communications they provide?"

THE MOST POPULAR RESPONSE **(40%)** FROM EMPLOYEES WAS THAT THEY **"WANT MORE THOUGHTFUL AND INSIGHTFUL DETAILS."**[2]

WHEN CEOs COMMUNICATE A COMPELLING, HIGH-LEVEL CHANGE STORY, THEY'RE **5.8 times more likely** TO SEE A SUCCESSFUL TRANSFORMATION WITHIN THEIR ORGANIZATIONS.[3]

SOURCE

[1] Axios, "The 2024 state of essential workplace communications," 2024

[2] Axios, "The 2023 state of essential workplace communications," 2023

[3] McKinsey & Company, "Losing from d one: Why even successful transformat fall short," Dec. 2021 Survey

PERCENTAGE OF LEADERS SURVEYED[4] THAT SAY THEY'VE SEEN THE FOLLOWING DIRECT RESULTS FROM EFFECTIVE INTERNAL COMMUNICATION:

45% Better employee engagement

42% Stronger teamwork and collaboration

40% Higher employee satisfaction scores

39% Greater team productivity

36% Better alignment with culture and values

32% Growing revenue or profits

32% Longer employee retention

30% Increased alignment with leadership vision

29% More independent decision-making

[4]Axios, "The 2024 state of essential workplace communications," 2024

TRANSPARENCY & WHY IT MATTERS

Q: In today's fast-paced, ever-changing business environment, what do you see as one of the most critical aspects of leadership communication?

A: Without a doubt, transparency. In a world where change is constant and uncertainty is high, employees crave transparency from their leaders. They want to know what's happening, why it's happening, and how it affects them. When leaders are transparent, it builds trust, reduces anxiety, and helps employees feel more connected to the organization's mission.

Q: But isn't there such a thing as being too transparent? Can't sharing too much information sometimes cause more problems than it solves?

A: It's a valid concern, and there are certainly times when complete transparency isn't appropriate, such as when dealing with confidential personnel issues or sensitive business dealings. But in general, I believe leaders err too far on the side of opacity. They withhold information out of fear of causing confusion or concern, but often, that lack of transparency does more harm than good.

Q: Can you give an example of how lack of transparency can backfire?

A: Absolutely. Imagine a company is going through a significant restructuring. Rumors are swirling, but leadership remains tight-lipped. Employees start to fill in the blanks themselves, often assuming the worst. Morale plummets, productivity suffers, and top talent starts to jump ship. Had leadership been upfront from the start about the reasons for the change and the expected outcomes, much of this could have been avoided.

Q: So how can leaders practice transparency in a way that benefits their organization?

A: First and foremost, make transparency a core value. Communicate to your team that open, honest communication is expected and valued. Then, look for opportunities to put transparency into practice:

- Share the "why" behind decisions, not simply the "what"
- Admit when you don't have all the answers
- Be upfront about challenges
- Regularly share updates, even if it's to say, "Here's what we know, here's what we don't know."
- Encourage questions and feedback, and respond honestly

Q: What would you say to a leader who's hesitant to be fully transparent?

A: I understand the hesitation. Transparency can feel risky, especially if you're used to playing things close to the vest. But in my experience, the benefits far outweigh the risks. When you're transparent, you build trust. You show your employees that you respect them enough to tell them the truth. And you create a culture of openness and authenticity that can be transformative for an organization.

Q: But my employees can't handle the truth!

A: Yes, they can! They might not like what you're sharing, but that's not the goal—that people like what you're communicating. As a leader, your goal should be for people to understand what you're communicating.

Q: Any final thoughts on transparency in leadership?

A: Transparency isn't a one-time act; it's a daily practice. It's not always easy, but it's always worth it. As a leader, your words and your actions set the tone for your entire organization. By embracing transparency, even when it's uncomfortable, you model the kind of leadership that inspires trust, engagement, and true commitment.

Reflection Questions

1. On a scale of 1-10, how would you rate your own transparency as a leader? What's one thing you could do to move that number higher?

2. Think of a leader you admire. How does that leader demonstrate transparency? What can you learn from their example?

3. What's one area where you could be more transparent starting today?

19

LESSONS FROM MY JOURNEY AS A HIGHER EDUCATION LEADER

Being named dean of the School of Journalism and Communication at the University of Oregon several years ago was a career highlight for me, then also a crash course in how to lead in difficult times.

While just settling in, I learned we faced an unexpected challenge—a significant budget deficit that had not been disclosed during the recruitment process. I was concerned yet determined to focus on the bright side. When I arrived in 2016, the school had considerable carry-forward funds, which I felt could be leveraged to balance the budget while we pursued important initiatives, including new production facilities. To face this tough moment, clear communication with the executive team, faculty, staff, and our advancement council was my top priority. My first step was to be transparent about the financial situation with faculty and staff. During an early meeting, we openly discussed the deficit and the plan to address it. I was transparent in explaining my desire to balance the budget and still achieve a surplus. The goal was to reduce expenses while advocating for additional investments in response to growing enrollment.

Throughout the process, I encouraged open communication and welcomed feedback from all the stakeholders. Many people appreciated having a voice, which built trust. Together, we brainstormed ideas and identified areas where costs could be reduced without compromising the quality of education and the student experience.

We made adjustments to ensure more efficient use of resources, more carefully monitored expenditures, and sought new revenue streams, mainly from summer and professional graduate programs. This strategic approach showed early signs of success, but we still needed solid support.

As the school began to stabilize financially, we tailored messages to resonate with each of our stakeholders. With faculty, I emphasized the long-term benefits of financial stability for academic programs. With students, I highlighted how the changes would enhance their educational experience.

CONTINUED...

While managing the financial situation, we also won the administration's support to hire specialized faculty and used donations and philanthropy toward scholarships for our students—a big win.

Naturally, the journey didn't end there, as all of higher education continues to confront competing demands for resources. In the academic year 2022-23, the consequences of the pandemic resulted in a new budget deficit. Again, continuous adaptation and acting on feedback earned trust and buy-in. Our leadership team and key stakeholders discussed the situation openly, and input was gathered throughout the process.

One of the most critical messages I shared was that we would do everything possible to address the deficit in ways that would be least disruptive to the school, and without undercutting our priorities. We wanted to maintain our newly revamped curriculum and additional production facilities on our two campuses. I reaffirmed our hope that further investment in production facilities would enhance career readiness and student success, making our undergraduate and graduate programs even more attractive and relevant.

Taking in feedback was critically important for the path forward as many concerns surfaced among the school community. In response, we revisited our initial financial strategies, identified additional cost-saving measures, and explored new opportunities to generate revenue. I assured the community that their feedback was not only heard, but would be acted upon. This iterative process of listening, recalibrating, and implementing new ideas became a hallmark of my leadership style.

The financial situation of the university and school continues to be in flux, as is the case for many higher education institutions today. We are fortunate that our administration is working with deans to increase funding for academic units, including our school.

What I've learned is just how important constant communication matters—and how much of a difference it can make in building the community's trust. Our leadership team is committed to communicating with context, transparency, and a willingness to act on feedback. Despite our financial challenges, we've been able to advocate for more courses and position our programs for continued success.

My experience has underscored that the measure of greatness for leaders has to be how they respond to the tough moments, not just the good times. Our leaders and our entire community continue to:

Rise to the occasion

Collaborate to allow us to meet the moment

Build a stronger program, one I'm *extremely proud to lead*

THE MODERN LEADERS

JUAN-CARLOS MOLLEDA, PH.D.

EDWIN L. ARTZT DEAN & PROFESSOR, UNIVERSITY OF OREGON SCHOOL OF JOURNALISM AND COMMUNICATION

CHANCES ARE YOU WAIT TOO LONG TO COMMUNICATE

You've been there—wanting to be transparent but hesitating to share information, thinking you need more time to gather facts or gain additional clarity. But here's the truth: That hesitation is costing you more than you realize. Your silence speaks volumes, and not in a good way.

The Dangerous Information Vacuum

While you're waiting to communicate, something critical happens: An information vacuum fills up, whether you want it to or not. Think of it like this—if you're not proactively sharing information, the grapevine is communicating for you. And trust me, that grapevine is excellent at perpetuating misinformation and myths that you'll later spend valuable time trying to clean up.

The Real Costs of Delayed Communication

When leaders wait to communicate, they trigger a cascade of organizational challenges:

- **Confusion:** Employees are left wondering and guessing
- **Miscommunication:** Rumors start to spread and take on a life of their own
- **Disengagement:** Your team feels disconnected and undervalued
- **Increased Perceived Workload:** Uncertainty creates mental exhaustion
- **Rampant Rumor Mill:** Speculation becomes the primary source of "information"

Why Employees Crave Transparent Communication

Your team doesn't expect you to have all the answers. In fact, they'd be suspicious if you claimed you did. What they want is simple:

- What you know
- What you don't know
- What you're working on finding out
- Proactive myth-busting

The 3 + 1 Communication Approach

When communicating during times of change, think of it as a **"3 + 1"** strategy:

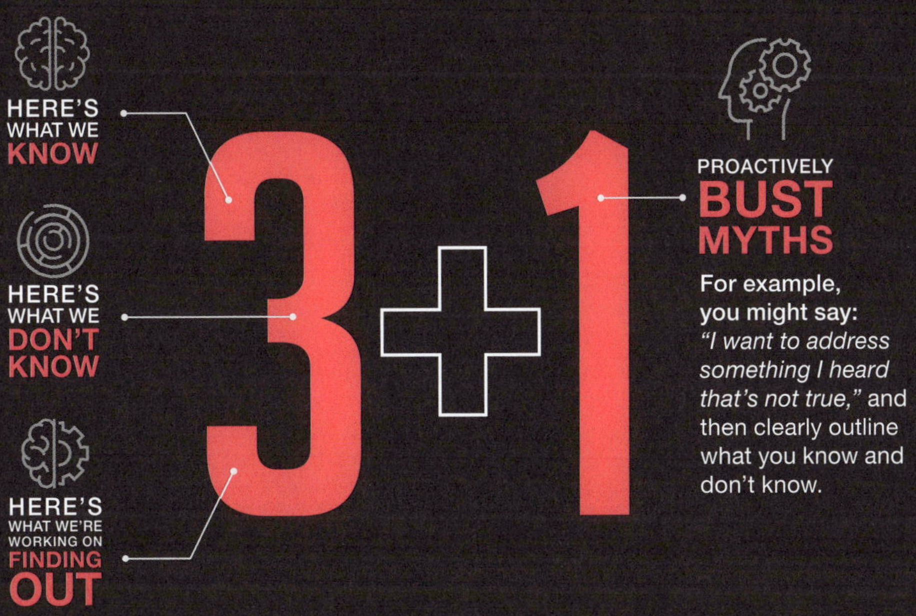

Remember that fear of imperfect communication often holds us back from sharing information when our teams need it most. The reality is, your willingness to communicate early and often—even when you don't have all the answers—builds trust and demonstrates respect for your employees. When you make transparent communication a priority, you create an environment where people feel valued, informed, and equipped to do their best work. The choice is yours: You can either fill the vacuum with clear, intentional messages that unite your team, or let the grapevine do the communicating for you. In the end, exceptional leadership means having the courage to share what you know, when you know it, and bringing your team along with you on the journey. The path forward is clear—start communicating sooner rather than later. Your team will thank you for it.

WHAT IS EFFECTIVE COMMUNICATION ANYWAY?

Think back to the last time you were moved by a leader's message. Perhaps it was a town hall that left you feeling inspired or a one-on-one conversation that gave you perfect clarity about your role. What made those moments so powerful?

The answer might surprise you. Despite what many think, effective communication isn't about being the most polished speaker or writing the most elegant emails. At its core, effective communication is about creating shared understanding that moves people to action.

Connecting with Your Audience

Exceptional leaders recognize that successful communication hinges on how well their message resonates with their audience. It's not about what you say, but rather what your listeners hear, understand, and act upon.

Imagine this scenario: You draft what you believe is the perfect announcement about a new company initiative. However, if your employees walk away confused about how it affects them or why they should care, the communication has missed the mark—no matter how well-crafted the message was.

Three Elements of Effective Communication

The most successful leaders focus on three essential elements:

1. Context First, Content Second

- Paint the big picture before diving into details
- Help people understand the "why" behind decisions
- Connect today's message to yesterday's conversations and tomorrow's goals

2. Audience at the Center

- Consider what your audience needs to know, feel, and do
- Answer the critical question: "What's in it for me?"
- Adapt your message based on who you're speaking to

3. Two-Way Understanding

- Create opportunities for dialogue
- Listen actively and check for understanding
- Be open to questions and feedback

Making It Real: A Meaningful Approach

Consider two leaders announcing the same project. The first dives straight into deadlines and deliverables. The second starts by sharing why the project matters:

"We're embarking on an initiative that will transform how our customers experience our brand and how our team delivers exceptional service. This is more than a new platform; it's an opportunity for each of us to make a lasting impact. Before we discuss timelines and action steps, let's first understand the significance of what we're creating together and the vital role you play in making it happen."

The second approach is effective because it provides meaningful context that helps employees see the larger purpose behind their daily work.

Quick Self-Assessment

Ask yourself these questions to gauge your communication effectiveness:

- Do I know what action I want to drive and did I include that in my communications?
- Do I regularly check how my messages are being received and understood?
- When communicating change, do I start with context or jump straight to details?
- How often do I create opportunities for two-way dialogue?
- Do I consider my audience's perspective when crafting messages?

Moving Forward

Effective communication isn't a natural gift—it's a skill that can be developed with intention and practice.

In the next section, we'll explore why context has become more important than ever in today's workplace, and how you can provide it in ways that resonate with your team.

WHAT'S THE CONTEXT ON THE IMPORTANCE OF CONTEXT?

As leaders, we often underestimate the power of context in our communication. We think that if we share the right information, our message will be heard and understood. But the reality is, without the proper context, even the most well-crafted message can fall flat.

Understanding Context

So, what exactly is context? In simple terms, context is the background information that helps your audience make sense of your message. It's the lens through which they view and interpret what you're saying. Think about it like a map at an airport. To understand where you are and where you need to go, you first need that big picture layout. That's context.

The Importance of Context in Today's Business Environment

In today's fast-paced, constantly changing business environment, providing context has become more critical than ever. Employees are bombarded with information from all directions, and without the right context, it's easy for important messages to get lost in the noise.

Consider a major transformation, like a company restructuring. If you simply announce the change without explaining the reasoning behind it, employees will likely feel confused, anxious, and possibly even resistant. But if you take the time to provide context—the market conditions that necessitated the change, the competitive landscape, or the long-term vision—suddenly, the change makes sense. Employees can see how it fits into the bigger picture and are more likely to get on board.

Creating a Shared Understanding

Providing context is also key to creating a shared understanding across your organization. Each of us comes to the workplace with our own individual context based on our background, experiences, and perceptions. As leaders, part of our job is to create a shared organizational context that everyone can relate to. When you connect the dots between your message and what your audience already knows, you help them see how it's relevant to them.

Putting Context into Practice

So how can you start incorporating more context into your communications? Start by always answering the "why" behind your message. Don't focus on the "what" and the "how"—explain the reasons behind decisions and how they tie into the bigger picture.

Use storytelling to help illustrate your points and make them more relatable. And most importantly, put yourself in your audience's shoes. What background information do they need to "get" what you're saying?

Reflection Questions

1. Think about a recent communication from leadership. Did it include the right amount of context? How could it have been improved?

2. Before your next communication, ask yourself: What does my audience already know about this topic? What background information do they need to fully understand my message?

3. Practice storytelling to help provide context. What anecdotes or examples can you share to illustrate your key points?

con • text

/käntekst/ ***n.***

1. the circumstances that form the setting for an event, statement, or idea, and in terms of which it can be fully understood and assessed.

"the decision was taken within the context of planned cuts in spending."

A COMMON LEADERSHIP PITFALL

As leaders, we often fall into a common trap when it comes to communication: We communicate from our own perspective, rather than considering the perspective of our audience. It's an easy mistake to make. After all, we're the ones with the information, the insights, the big picture view. We know what we want to say, and we assume that our audience will understand and interpret our message the same way we do.

But here's the thing: our audience doesn't live in our heads. They don't have access to all the context and background knowledge that we do. And, when we fail to consider their perspective, our communication often falls flat.

Seeing Through Your Audience's Eyes

Effective communication is not about what you say; it's about what your audience hears and understands. To really get your message across, you need to put yourself in your audience's shoes. What do they already know about this topic? What are their concerns and priorities? What questions might they have?

Imagine you're announcing a major organizational change. From your perspective, this change is necessary and exciting. You've been involved in the planning process and you can see all the benefits it will bring. But your employees may not have that context. Their immediate thoughts might be: "What does this mean for my job? How will my day-to-day work change? Why is this happening now?" If you don't address these questions upfront, you're likely to face resistance and confusion.

The Power of Empathy

We've already talked extensively about the importance of empathy in the context of understanding what others might be feeling. When you communicate with empathy, you show your audience that you understand and care about their needs and concerns. You anticipate the questions they might have and proactively address them. You use language that resonates with them, rather than defaulting to corporate jargon.

Empathetic communication builds trust and rapport. It shows your employees that you're not broadcasting information, but that you're engaged in a dialogue. And when employees feel that you're thinking about them and their needs, they're far more likely to be receptive to your message.

Strategies for Audience-Centric Communication

So how can you shift your communication style to be more audience-centric? Here are a few strategies to try:

- **Know your audience:** Take time to understand who you're communicating with. What are their roles, their challenges, and their goals? What information do they need from you?
- **Put yourself in their shoes:** Before crafting your message, imagine how it might land with your audience. What might they think and feel upon hearing this news? What questions will they have?
- **Use inclusive language:** Avoid jargon and corporate-speak. Use language that is clear, concise, and relatable to your audience.
- **Encourage dialogue:** Don't broadcast information—invite questions and feedback. Show your audience that their input is valued.
- **Check for understanding:** Don't assume your message has landed. Ask questions to gauge understanding and clarify any confusion.

Communicating from your audience's perspective takes practice and intentionality. But it's a skill that will serve you well as a leader. When you make the effort to understand and empathize with your audience, you build the trust and engagement that is essential for driving results.

Reflection Questions

1. Think about a recent communication you delivered. Did you consider your audience's perspective? What could you have done differently?

2. Before your next communication, take time to put yourself in your audience's shoes. What questions and concerns might they have? How can you address these proactively?

3. Practice active listening in your next conversation. Focus on understanding the other person's perspective before sharing your own.

20

DEVELOPING A SENSE OF TRUST IN A TIME OF CRISIS

In early 2020, the COVID-19 virus emerged out of nowhere. It spread rapidly, leaving people around the world in a state of shock and disbelief. Sadly, many died.

In the United States, as misinformation about COVID-19 spread, health care systems communicated what they knew. Communicating was challenging because researchers regularly were discovering new information. At the same time, researchers worked tirelessly to develop vaccines.

Health care systems in the United States began planning how to roll out vaccines in their communities. At Cone Health, where I am the chief marketing and communications officer, we initially planned for community members to come to our facilities for their vaccines. During one of our leadership team meetings as we were talking about the vaccine rollout, I shared that not everyone in our community was anxious to get vaccinated—particularly in minority communities.

VACCINE HESITATION IS ROOTED IN HISTORY

Here is why. History records that African Americans have not always been treated fairly and ethically in health studies. Perhaps the best example of a study that did not bode well for African American males is the Tuskegee syphilis study. This study was started in 1932 by the US Public Health Service.

Over the course of many years, an estimated 400 African American males from Tuskegee, Alabama, who had syphilis were recruited for this study.

Some years later, when antibiotics became available for treatment in the 1940s, these same African Americans were denied access to those drugs for treatment. By the time the study was ended in 1972, more than 100 had died from advanced syphilis.[1]

Research shows that the participants never were asked for their consent to take part in the study. Nor were the participants specifically told about the details of the study. They also did not volunteer for the project. Instead, they were "deceived into thinking they were 'getting free treatment from government doctors for a serious disease.'"[1]

The Tuskegee experiment is one example of how minorities in the United States view new treatments, including vaccines. Against this context, we realized at Cone Health that we needed a different approach to leading and communicating about the new COVID-19 vaccines. Our leadership had to be authentic to establish trust among the racial and ethnic groups whom we are privileged to serve.

AUTHENTIC LEADERSHIP YIELDS TRUST

Among leadership scholars, there is more than one definition of authentic leadership.[2]

For the purposes of this discussion, we will define authentic leadership as an interpersonal process, resulting not from the leader's efforts alone but also from the response of followers.

Authentic leadership emerges from the interactions between leaders and followers. Authentic leadership is a reciprocal process because leaders affect followers and followers affect leaders.[2]

Authentic leadership was a non-negotiable for us as we communicated to our community members about the value of getting vaccinated.

CONTINUED...

20

Here's a summary of what authentic leadership looked like for us:

1 **WE LEANED INTO THE FACT THAT WE SERVE A DIVERSE COMMUNITY** with different backgrounds, experiences, and perspectives. This community needed multiple ways to receive information about the new vaccines.

2 **OUR CLINICIANS (DOCTORS, NURSES, ETC.) WERE AMONG THE FIRST TO GET VACCINATED,** allowing them to authentically communicate with community members that they had received the vaccine and it was safe.

3 **WE PROVIDED VACCINE ACCESS OPTIONS.** Community members could visit our facilities, and we also partnered with houses of worship and community organizations to bring vaccines directly to them.

4 **WE HELD VIRTUAL TOWN HALLS WHERE COMMUNITY MEMBERS ENGAGED WITH CLINICIANS TO ASK QUESTIONS,** debunk myths, and encourage vaccination. This effort was successful.

5 **WE ENSURED THAT OUR CLINICIANS WHO WERE LEADING OUR VIRTUAL TOWN HALLS REFLECTED OUR DIVERSE COMMUNITY.** Feedback showed that people appreciated engaging with clinicians who looked like them.

CONCLUSION

In today's dynamic business environment, a hallmark of effective leadership is the ability to communicate with context. Communicating with context answers questions that could stand in the way of two or more people working together to achieve shared goals.

Communicating with context is a skill of authentic leadership. Authentic leadership is a learned behavior that can occur when two or more people interact with each other. Authentic leadership can be successful when leaders and followers agree to be open and honest with each other.

At the heart of authentic leadership is a shared commitment to communicating with context so that a sense of trust can be developed. This includes meeting people where they are—literally and figuratively—so that context can be established and trust can be developed. How committed are you to being an authentic leader who communicates with context?

CHUCK WALLINGTON, PH.D.

EXECUTIVE VICE PRESIDENT & CHIEF MARKETING & COMMUNICATIONS OFFICER, CONE HEALTH

SOURCES

[1]Hesse-Biber, S.N. (2017). The practice of qualitative research (3rd ed.). Thousand Oaks, CA: SAGE.

[2]Northouse, P.G. (2016). Leadership Theory and Practice (7th ed.). Los Angeles: SAGE Publications, Inc.

YOU ASKED FOR FEEDBACK: THE MISTAKE TOO MANY LEADERS THEN MAKE

As a leader, you know that actively seeking feedback from your team is a powerful way to gain valuable insights and drive meaningful change. After all, your employees are on the front lines every day, and their perspectives can shed light on challenges and opportunities that may not be immediately apparent.

However, simply gathering feedback isn't enough. The real work begins once you have that input in hand. Too often, leaders make the mistake of not acting on the feedback they receive, leaving employees feeling unheard and disengaged. To leverage the power of employee feedback, you must communicate clearly about how you're putting their ideas into action. This means closing the loop with your team:

1. You're implementing their solution, and sharing why it makes sense for the business.

2. You're adopting a modified version of their idea and the rationale behind that.

3. You've decided not to move forward with their suggestion with an explanation of your reasoning.

In each case, it's crucial to cover not simply what you're doing, but why you've chosen that path. Sharing your thought process helps your team understand how you approach decisions and empowers them to bring you even more relevant, impactful ideas in the future.

Don't forget to highlight where the winning idea originated and share appreciation with the employee who brought it forward. When your employees see that their feedback leads to tangible change, they'll be far more likely to share their perspective in the future. If they perceive you're not listening, you might find silence in your future.

Your team is ready and willing to help drive your organization forward. Are you prepared to hear them—and more importantly, to put their feedback into action?

The next time you ask your employees to share their thoughts, remember that your most important work is what comes next. By closing the loop and taking meaningful steps based on their input, you won't just build a stronger organization—you'll cultivate a team that feels heard, valued, and engaged in driving your strategy forward.

THE 8 KEY QUESTIONS: UNDERSTANDING YOUR EMPLOYEES' FUNDAMENTAL NEEDS

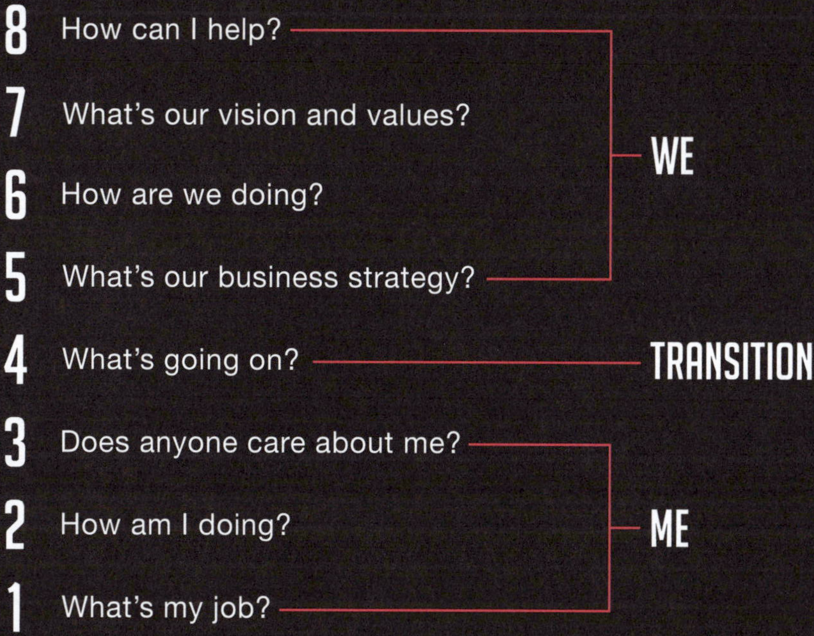

With all the change in the workplace, understanding and addressing your employees' fundamental needs has never been more critical. Whether voiced aloud or kept private, there are eight essential questions on employees' minds, especially during times of change and uncertainty. These questions form a natural progression from basic individual needs to higher-level organizational engagement.

The Foundation: Understanding Human Motivation

The 8 Key Questions framework is grounded in Maslow's Hierarchy of Needs, the foundational psychological theory that explains human motivation. Just as individuals must satisfy basic physiological and safety needs before pursuing higher aspirations, employees must have their fundamental workplace needs met before they can fully engage with broader organizational goals. The 8 Key Questions model was adapted from one of the leading pioneers in internal communications, Roger D'Aprix.

The Three Levels of Employee Questions

Me-Focused Questions

The first level addresses immediate personal concerns that form the foundation of workplace security and well-being. These questions must be answered before employees can focus on broader organizational matters:

1. "What's my job?"

2. "How am I doing?"

3. "Does anyone care about me?"

You could argue, by the way, that there's a question 0: "Do I have a job?" but I like to think positively.

The Transition Question

The bridge between personal and organizational focus:

4. "What's going on?"

Once employees feel taken care of, they're able to look outside of themselves and notice what's happening in the organization. That's when they ask, "What's going on?" "In that other function?" "In that part of the world?" "On that major project?"

We-Focused Questions

Once basic needs are met, employees can engage with larger organizational goals:

5. "What's our strategy?"

6. "How are we doing at our strategy?"

7. "What are our vision and values?"

These questions are very much like the me-focused questions but bigger, and at the organizational level.

Finally, there's question 8:

8. "How can I help?"

This is all about engagement. How powerful would it be for 10-15% more of our people to say, "I can do more," or "I want a stretch assignment," or "How can I help our team thrive even more?"

The Power of Progression

Understanding this progression is crucial for leaders. When change occurs—whether it's organizational restructuring, new leadership, or external challenges—employees naturally return to the bottom of the pyramid with the me-focused questions.

This isn't a sign of selfishness or disengagement; it's a fundamental human response to uncertainty. I think, literally, "What about me?" "Does this change impact me, and if so, how?"

That's when leaders play a critical role in helping employees move through the progression back to the top. Otherwise, employees can get lost in the typical change curve and what's often called the Valley of Despair.

This is a black hole of "Woe is me," or "I don't agree with this change," or "I don't care for this organization anymore." Bottom line—when employees get caught in this trough, work stops, slows, or gets interrupted, and disengagement happens.

Creating a Supporting Environment

To help employees move through these questions effectively:

1. Acknowledge the Natural Cycle: Recognize that during times of change, employees will cycle back to me-focused questions

2. Provide Clear Communication: Address basic questions quickly, directly, and repeatedly

3. Build Trust Through Consistency: Maintain regular check-ins and open dialogue

4. Support Individual Growth: Help employees see their role in the context of this change and the larger organizational success

REMEMBER:
Addressing these questions isn't a one-time event but an ongoing process. As your organization evolves and faces new challenges, employees will naturally cycle through these questions again and again. That means this is an ongoing dialogue about your organization's transformation and the critical role every employee plays.

THE CHANGE CURVE & VALLEY OF DESPAIR: A LEADER'S GUIDE

The Change Curve, based on Elisabeth Kübler-Ross's work[1], maps the emotional journey people experience during significant change. Understanding this curve helps leaders anticipate reactions and provide appropriate support throughout the change process.

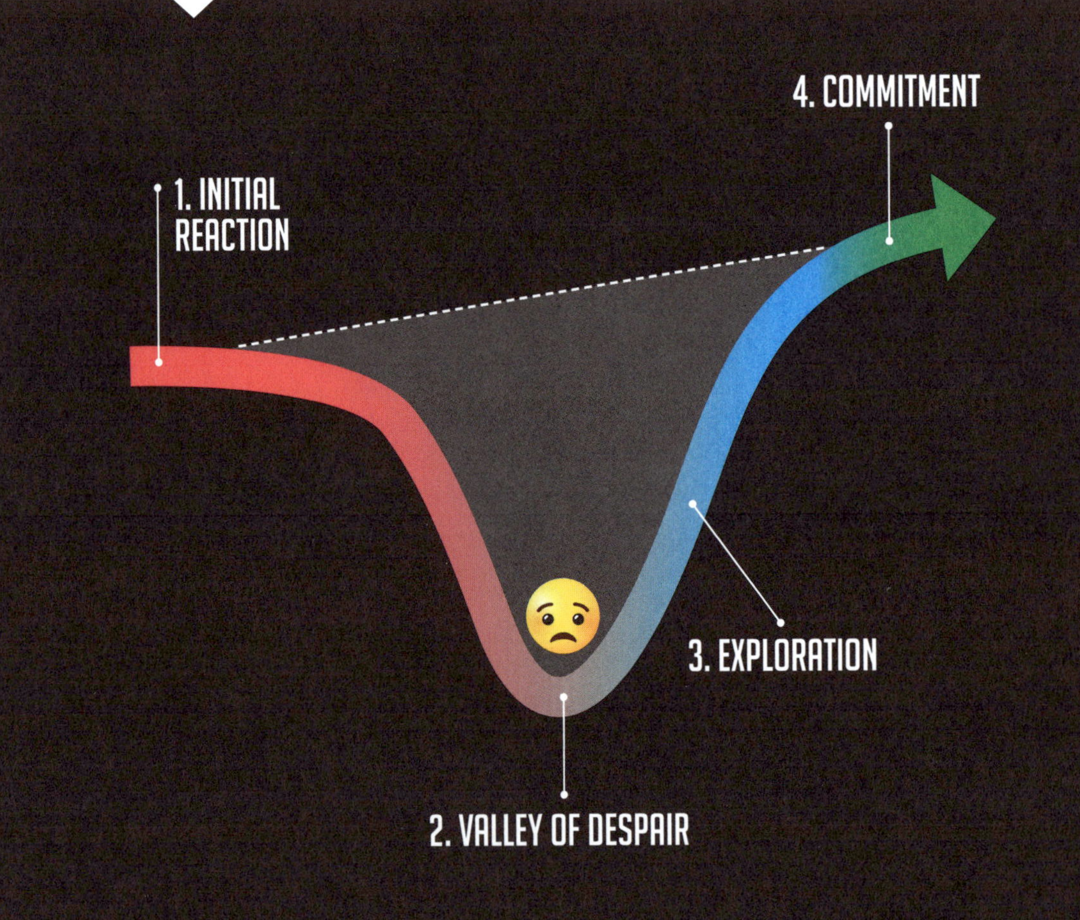

The Journey Through Change

The curve typically follows four stages:

1. Initial Reaction: When change is announced, people react with either shock/denial or excitement/anticipation.

2. Valley of Despair: As reality sets in, people experience confusion, frustration, and fear. Performance and morale often hit their lowest point here as people struggle with new expectations and letting go of familiar ways.

3. Exploration: People gradually begin testing new approaches and understanding the benefits of the change.

4. Commitment: Finally, people embrace the change, integrate new behaviors, and return to (and often exceed) previous performance levels.

[1]Elisabeth Kübler-Ross, On Death and Dying, 1969. While originally developed to explain the five stages of grief, her work has been widely adapted to understand reactions to significant organizational change.

Leadership Implications

The Valley of Despair is where individual employees are most at risk of disengagement. Leaders can help each team member by:

- Having regular one-on-one conversations to understand personal concerns
- Answering the employee's me-focused questions about their role and future
- Connecting their work to the bigger picture of organizational success
- Providing specific, timely feedback about their contributions
- Creating opportunities for them to participate in shaping the change
- Identifying and removing obstacles that might prevent their success
- Recognizing their progress and celebrating their individual wins

Success requires recognizing that the Valley of Despair is temporary and natural. When leaders support employees as individuals rather than as a group, they can help each person maintain engagement and emerge stronger from the change experience.

FINE-TUNING YOUR LEADERSHIP COMMUNICATION

Not all communication is created equal. Just as a musician must tune their instrument to create beautiful music, leaders must calibrate their communication style to effectively reach and engage their audience.

What Is Communication Calibration?

Communication calibration is the art of adjusting your communication style to meet the needs and preferences of your audience. It's about understanding that different people have different communication needs and that a one-size-fits-all approach rarely works.

Some employees may prefer detailed, data-driven explanations, while others may respond better to big-picture, visionary statements. Some may appreciate a direct, no-nonsense approach, while others may need more empathy and encouragement. As a leader, it's your job to recognize and respond to these different needs.

Why Calibration Matters

When you calibrate your communication, you demonstrate that you value and respect your audience. You show that you're not just interested in broadcasting your own message, but that you're committed to ensuring that message is received and understood.

Moreover, calibrated communication is simply more effective. When you tailor your message to your audience, you're more likely to get your point across, to inspire action, and to achieve your goals.

Strategies for Calibrating Your Communication

So how can you start calibrating your communication? Here are a few strategies to consider:

1. Know your team: Take time to understand the individuals on your team. What are their communication styles? What motivates and inspires them? What challenges are they facing?

2. Listen actively: Don't wait for your turn to speak—really listen to what your employees are saying. Pay attention to their words, their tone, and their body language.

3. Ask questions: Don't assume you know what your audience needs. Ask them directly: "How can I best support you?" "What information do you need from me?" "What's your preferred communication style?"

4. Adapt your style: Based on what you learn, adapt your communication style. This might mean providing more context, using more visual aids, checking in more frequently, or adjusting your tone.

5. Seek feedback: Regularly ask your team for feedback on your communication. What's working well? What could be improved? Be open to constructive criticism and willing to make changes.

Leadership communication isn't a one-and-done proposition. It's an ongoing process of calibration, adjustment, and improvement. By continually tuning in to your audience and adapting your approach, you can become a more effective, more impactful leader.

Reflection Questions

1. Think about your own communication style. Do you tend to use the same approach with everyone? How might you start to calibrate your style?

2. Consider each member of your team. What do you know about their communication preferences? What could you do to better understand and meet their needs?

3. Recall a time when a communication didn't land as intended. In hindsight, how might calibrating your approach have helped?

ELEVATING ORGANIZATIONAL COMMUNICATION:

A GUIDE FOR SENIOR LEADERSHIP TEAMS

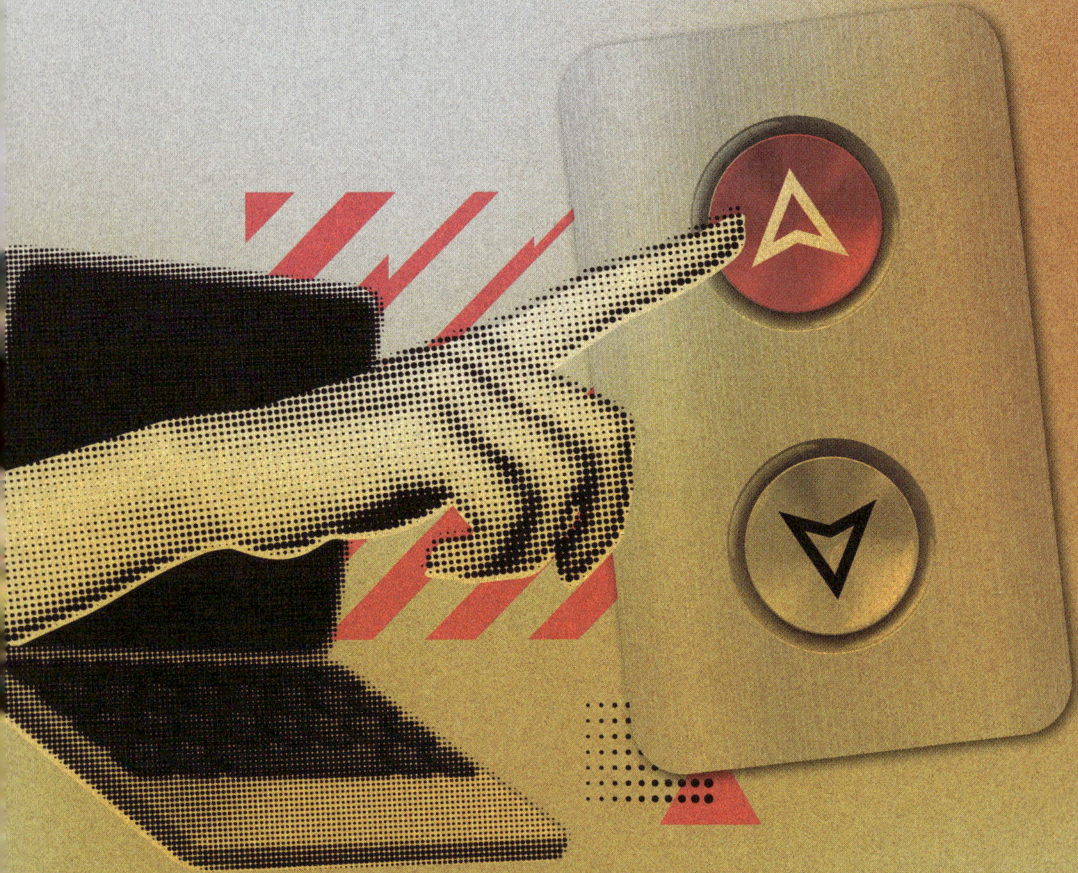

As a senior leadership team, your approach to communication context sets the foundation for organizational clarity, alignment, and high performance. When context becomes a strategic priority—rather than an afterthought—you create a powerful lever for employee engagement and collective success. Here are the key actions you can take to make communication context a competitive advantage:

1 Establish Context as a Leadership Imperative

Why This Matters: Teams that proactively share context transform employee understanding from passive compliance to active commitment. When employees understand the "why" behind initiatives, engagement and performance soar.

Leadership Team Actions:

- Create a comprehensive context-sharing framework for major organizational initiatives as part of an overall enterprise-wide narrative
- Develop a communication dashboard that tracks context transparency
- Train leaders on the art of meaningful context delivery
- Link context directly to business outcomes and strategic goals
- Measure the impact of communication on organizational performance

2 Design Systematic Context-Sharing Mechanisms

Why This Matters: Consistent, structured context sharing becomes the lifeblood of organizational understanding. Build communication transparency into your standard business rhythms.

Leadership Team Actions:

- Implement regular all-hands meetings with deep-dive context sessions
- Create quarterly strategic context briefings for all employees
- Establish monthly leadership listening sessions
- Design storytelling workshops to help leaders communicate context effectively

3 Break Down Communication Silos

Why This Matters: Siloed communication fragments organizational understanding. Leaders must work to create transparent, interconnected communication channels.

Leadership Team Actions:

- Create cross-departmental communication forums
- Develop communication platforms that enable real-time context sharing
- Implement shadowing programs to enhance inter-departmental understanding

CONTINUED

ELEVATING ORGANIZATIONAL COMMUNICATION:

A GUIDE FOR SENIOR LEADERSHIP TEAMS

4 Build Organizational Context-Sharing Capabilities

Why This Matters: Effective context communication is a learned skill that requires intentional development at all leadership levels.

Leadership Team Actions:

- Invest in comprehensive communication training programs
- Create context-sharing toolkits for managers
- Develop mentoring programs focused on communication excellence
- Establish best-practice libraries for contextual communication
- Include communication skills in leadership competency models

5 Embed Context into Talent Development

Why This Matters: When context sharing becomes integral to your talent systems, it transforms from an occasional practice to an organizational superpower.

Leadership Team Actions:

- Include context-sharing skills in leadership performance assessments
- Develop communication effectiveness metrics
- Integrate contextual communication into onboarding programs
- Reward leaders who excel at providing meaningful organizational context
- Create career development paths that prioritize communication skills

6 Create Accountability for Contextual Communication

Why This Matters: What gets measured gets prioritized. Establish clear expectations and metrics for communication effectiveness.

Leadership Team Actions:

- Set specific context-sharing goals for each leadership level
- Track communication transparency and depth
- Conduct regular employee surveys on communication effectiveness
- Include communication context in business reviews
- Share communication analytics across the organization

QUESTIONS FOR YOUR NEXT SENIOR TEAM MEETING

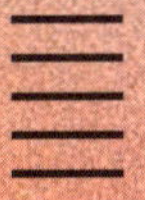

1. How effectively are we currently sharing organizational context?
2. Where are the biggest gaps in our communication approach?
3. What systems could we create to make context sharing more consistent?
4. How are we measuring the impact of our communication efforts?
5. What's one communication practice we could improve starting tomorrow?

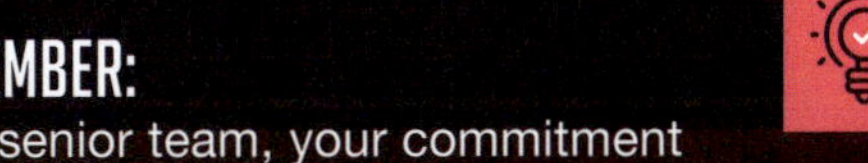

REMEMBER:

As a senior team, your commitment to sharing meaningful context sets the standard for your entire organization. When you move from sporadic updates to strategic, transparent communication, you create the conditions for unprecedented organizational alignment and performance.

ACCESS POPULAR COMMUNICATION RESOURCES

FREE

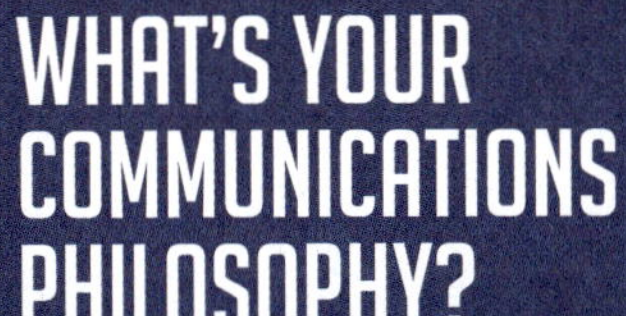

WHAT'S YOUR COMMUNICATIONS PHILOSOPHY?

Tool

TAKE 5 TO COMMUNICATE WELL

Tool

COMMUNICATE IN TIMES OF CHANGE

Tool

5 Ws AND AN H: A GUIDE TO COMMUNICATING VIRTUALLY ANYTHING IN BUSINESS

Blog

5. CONNECT STRATEGY TO EMPLOYEE GROWTH

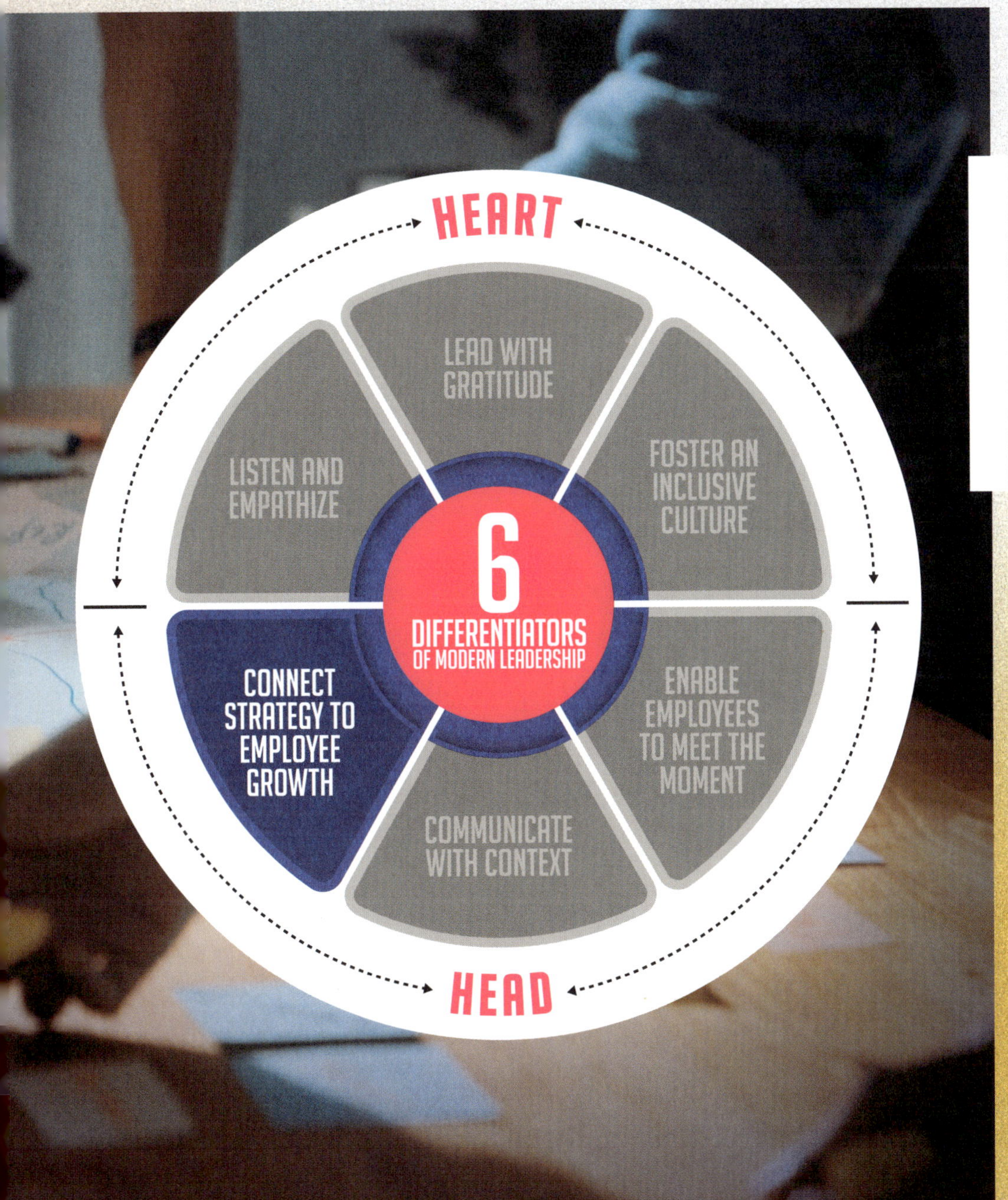
HEART
LEAD WITH GRATITUDE
LISTEN AND EMPATHIZE
FOSTER AN INCLUSIVE CULTURE
6
DIFFERENTIATORS
OF MODERN LEADERSHIP
CONNECT STRATEGY TO EMPLOYEE GROWTH
ENABLE EMPLOYEES TO MEET THE MOMENT
COMMUNICATE WITH CONTEXT
HEAD

"Where do I fit into this company's future?"

It's a question every employee asks themselves, whether they voice it or not. They want to know if their career aspirations align with the organization's direction. They wonder if developing new skills will open doors for growth. They seek assurance that investing their time and talent here will lead somewhere meaningful.

As leaders, one of our most critical responsibilities is helping employees see their place in the organization's future. This goes beyond simply sharing the corporate strategy or conducting annual reviews. It's about

CREATING GENUINE CONNECTIONS BETWEEN EACH PERSON'S CAREER JOURNEY AND THE ORGANIZATION'S PATH FORWARD.

When employees can clearly envision their future with your organization, everything changes. They become more invested in their own development. They actively seek opportunities to grow new capabilities. Most importantly, they see themselves as key players in building the organization's future, not solely passengers along for the ride.

In this chapter, we'll explore how to help employees reach their full potential. We'll cover aligning individual career goals with organizational needs, crafting impactful development plans, facilitating candid growth conversations, and making development part of daily work, not solely annual reviews.

The most successful leaders recognize that connecting employees to their future in the organization is an ongoing commitment to helping each person grow alongside the business. And in doing so, you're even better positioned to activate your company's strategy through your engaged employees. Let's explore how to make that happen.

WHAT THE RESEARCH SAYS

ORGANIZATIONS THAT HAVE MADE A STRATEGIC INVESTMENT IN EMPLOYEE DEVELOPMENT REPORT

11%

greater profitability

AND ARE ***TWICE*** AS LIKELY TO RETAIN THEIR EMPLOYEES.[1]

EMPLOYEES WHO USE THEIR STRENGTHS DAILY ARE

six times

MORE LIKELY TO BE ENGAGED AT WORK.[2]

SOURCE

[1]Desimone, R. (December, 2019) Improve Work Performance With a Focus on Employee Development. Gallup.

[2]Sorenson, S. (2014) How Employees' Strengths Make Your Company Stronger. Gallup Business Journal.

Millennials are more likely to STAY in their current role

WHEN PRACTICES OF STRUCTURED MENTORING AND STRATEGIC LEADERSHIP ARE CONSISTENTLY OBSERVED.[3]

[3]Younas, M., & Bari, M. W. (2020). The relationship between talent management practices and retention of generation 'Y' employees: mediating role of competency development. Economic Research-Ekonomska Istraživanja, 33(1), 1330–1353.

21

"AVERAGE IS OVER. MEDIOCRITY IS A DEATH SENTENCE."

GARY RYAN BLAIR, CAREER COACH

One late evening when I headed Ketchum Chicago, I was leaving the office and spotted recently hired consumer intern Myreete (Wolford) Stanforth sitting on the floor of the business development office busily pasting artwork on storyboards needed the following morning for a new business pitch. When I asked what she was doing, Myreete explained she made it a routine before leaving the office each night to stop by the offices of busy-looking people to offer her assistance. At that moment, I predicted she would be a standout success in the agency world.

Now, 11 years later, Myreete is based in London, where she serves as Ketchum's head of global markets and marketing. Myreete led with heart and passion throughout her active college career at the University of Alabama and in each of her Ketchum positions. "You have to be passionate, present, and prepared in everything you do," Myreete explained. "Sharing your passions allows leaders—and peers—to know when to best tap you. Being present—and being visible—is the most important factor in leaders remembering your name when considering opportunities. Finally, ensuring your day-to-day work is completed (and without error) will allow you to be prepared to say 'yes!' without delay. Live ready for opportunity."

Explaining how her early volunteering efforts at Ketchum shaped her career, Myreete said: "I'd argue that being present is the most important as you're able to pop your head into an office to learn about a project, hear an issue you might be able to fix, or raise your hand with extra time and showcase your skillset. I did this for a pitch once—I made a pre-send video to amplify our pitch and proofed an RFP submission. I fell in love with the process so much I made it my entire career. I also did this to move to London from Chicago, where I made an 8-page business case on how I could benefit the UK office in my request to transfer. That request coincided with a business need, which afforded me the new global position."

Myreete also credits her "big-picture mentors" who taught her that great ideas are more likely to be considered if they align with the larger business strategy.

"Many will support you throughout, but no one will do it for you," Myreete asserts.

"BE HUMBLE IN THE PROCESS, BUT DON'T APOLOGIZE FOR THE SUCCESS. CAPITALIZE ON GOOD TIMING AND GIVE GRATITUDE TO GREAT LEADERSHIP."

Another young communications leader learned how to become indispensable through his effective use of social media.

When he decided to move on from his career in the Marines where he was based at Camp Pendelton, California, Luis Agostini decided to return to the Midwest and complete his undergraduate degree at DePaul University. Despite being nearly 2,000 miles from Chicago, Luis turned to social media to lay the groundwork for his arrival on campus and his ensuing job search.

Before his arrival in the Windy City, Luis had already connected with key professors and started following and engaging through tweets with agency leaders. One of those leaders, Rick Murray, President of Edelman Chicago, was so impressed with his initiative that he invited Luis to join him for coffee to discuss potential internships. No internship transpired, but Rick hired Luis as a contractor at a far greater hourly rate than interns make.

During the next few years of his career at several premier Chicago agencies, Luis was known for readily volunteering

CONTINUED...

to help wherever needed. As a result, he learned key lessons that built on his 11 years of leadership observations in the Marines. Today, Luis loves and is passionate about his job as a public relations specialist for the Drug Enforcement Administration.

"LEADING WITH GRATITUDE MEANS EMBRACING THE MINDSET THAT YOU HAVE BEEN BLESSED WITH THE PRIVILEGE OF LEADERSHIP AND APPROACHING YOUR RESPONSIBILITIES AS A LEADER WITH THE MENTALITY THAT YOU 'GET' TO LEAD, NOT THAT YOU 'HAVE' TO LEAD."

Luis elaborates further: "This mindset can be contagious, as team members throughout the organization will feed off of the display of gratitude, which will ultimately reflect in the output and quality of the work performed."

Like Myreete, Luis also stresses the importance of creating an open, inclusive culture. His point: "Fostering an inclusive culture demands more than just recruiting a diverse representation of different backgrounds and life experiences but cultivating opportunities for employees from diverse and underrepresented backgrounds to participate, thrive, and advance in an organization. It also means creating space for the diverse employees to show up and celebrate their true selves, while embracing the organization's culture and identity."

While noting the importance of listening, empathizing, and continuous learning, Luis said his best supervisors fostered an environment that didn't punish mistakes or momentary failure.

"Employees, especially those with big ideas, opinions, and even constant pushbacks, can thrive and succeed when given the opportunity to manage their piece of a given project with proper guidance and resources—with minimal micromanagement," Luis explains. A final big plus is when leaders successfully connect strategy to employee growth.

Myreete and Luis exemplify the advice of career coach Gary Ryan Blair, who says:

"AVERAGE IS OVER. MEDIOCRITY IS A DEATH SENTENCE. YOU MUST EMBRACE THE FACT THAT FOR YOU TO REMAIN COMPETITIVE, RELEVANT, AND OF VALUE... YOU HAVE NO CHOICE BUT TO GO THE EXTRA MILE AND EXCEED EXPECTATIONS AT ALL TIMES."

RON CULP

LECTURER, DEPAUL UNIVERSITY | PRSA GOLD ANVIL AWARD & PAGE SOCIETY DISTINGUISHED SERVICE & HALL OF FAME AWARD RECIPIENT

WHY EMPLOYEES CARE ABOUT THEIR PLACE IN YOUR TALENT STRATEGY

Kendall, a mid-level manager at a global pharmaceutical company, shared this frustration in a recent focus group. "I'm doing good work," she said. "My team is delivering. But I have no idea if what I'm doing matters in the big picture. Am I developing the right skills? Is my department even going to exist in five years? Sometimes I wonder if I should be looking elsewhere."

Kendall's story isn't unique. It reflects a fundamental human need to see a future for ourselves in the organizations where we spend so much of our time and energy.

The Hidden Cost of Uncertainty

When employees can't see their place in your organization's future, several things happen:

1. They Disengage: Without a clear future, people invest less in the present

2. They Play It Safe: Uncertainty leads to conservative choices rather than innovation

3. They Look Elsewhere: Top performers seek organizations where they can envision their future

What Employees Really Want to Know

Here are five core questions that people need answered:

1. "How does my work contribute to our future success?"

2. "What skills should I be developing?"

3. "What opportunities exist for growth?"

4. "How will my role evolve as the organization changes?"

5. "Does leadership see my potential?"

The Leader's Role

As a leader, you play a crucial role in answering these questions through:

- **Creating Visibility:** Share career paths and growth opportunities openly
- **Connecting the Dots:** Help employees see how their current work builds future capabilities
- **Having Regular Conversations:** Make career discussions part of your routine

- **Sharing Success Stories:** Highlight examples of internal growth and development
- **Providing Clear Pathways:** Show multiple routes for advancement, both vertical and horizontal

Reflection Questions

Take a moment to consider:

1. When was the last time you discussed your team members' career aspirations?

2. How clearly can your employees articulate their future opportunities in your organization?

3. What one step could you take this week to better connect individual growth to organizational needs?

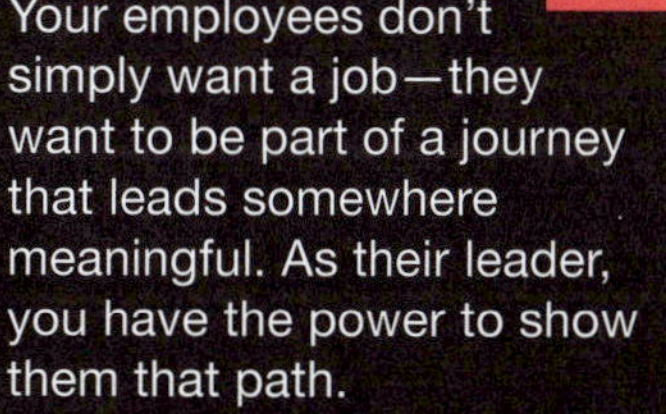

REMEMBER:
Your employees don't simply want a job—they want to be part of a journey that leads somewhere meaningful. As their leader, you have the power to show them that path.

MAKING STRATEGY REAL: A LEADER'S GUIDE TO CONSISTENT STRATEGIC COMMUNICATION

When employees can't see their future in your organization, it's often because they're missing a crucial piece of the puzzle: A clear understanding of where the organization is headed and how their career path fits into that journey.

One of the biggest traps leaders fall into is assuming that because they've shared the strategy once, employees can connect these dots themselves. The reality is that employees need to hear repeatedly not only what the strategy is and its natural evolution, but also the role they play in it and how it creates opportunities for their growth and development.

The 3C Framework for Strategic Communication

To make strategy real, use the "3C Framework":

Context

- Frame the bigger picture
- Explain the "why" behind decisions
- Connect initiatives to future goals

Clarity

- Use simple, jargon-free language
- Provide specific examples
- Break down complex concepts

Connection

- Link strategy to individual roles
- Show progress and impact
- Celebrate strategic wins

Making It Work: Your Weekly Communication Rhythm

Here's a practical approach to weaving strategy into your regular communications:

Monday Team Huddles

- Share one strategic priority for the week
- Connect team tasks to broader goals
- Address questions about direction

Wednesday Check-Ins

- Review progress on strategic initiatives
- Share success stories
- Identify and remove obstacles

Friday Wrap-Ups

- Celebrate strategic wins
- Preview next week's focus
- Reinforce key messages

The Power of Strategic Storytelling

Don't simply share data—share stories that bring strategy to life:

1. **Situation:** What was the challenge?
2. **Action:** What did we do?
3. **Strategic Link:** How did this support our strategy?
4. **Result:** What was the impact?
5. **Learning:** What did we discover?

Common Pitfalls to Avoid

1. The "One and Done" Trap

- Thinking one town hall or communication covers it
- Not reinforcing messages regularly
- Failing to connect daily work to strategy

2. The "Too Complex" Challenge

- Using technical jargon
- Overwhelming with details
- Missing emotional connection

3. The "Missing Link" Problem

- Not connecting strategy to individual roles
- Focusing on "what" without explaining "why"
- Skipping success stories

QUICK IMPLEMENTATION GUIDE

Start Tomorrow:

- Take 5 minutes in your next team meeting to share one strategic priority
- Ask each team member how their current project supports that priority
- Document and share one success story that illustrates strategy in action

2

Next Week:

- Review your recurring meeting agendas—add strategic connection points
- Create a simple one-page strategy summary to always connect back to
- Discuss strategy for 15 minutes at your check-ins with key team members

3

Next Month:

- Develop a communication calendar
- Build a library of strategic success stories
- Train your team leads on strategic messaging

SELF-ASSESSMENT QUESTIONS:

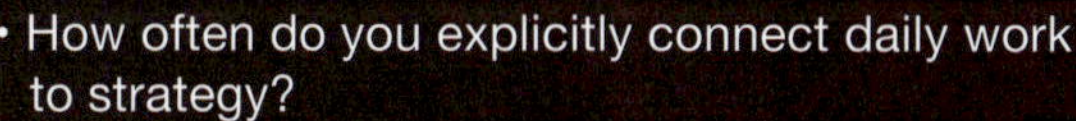

- How often do you explicitly connect daily work to strategy?
- Can your team members articulate how their work supports organizational goals?
- What's your process for gathering and sharing strategic success stories?
- How do you measure whether your strategic messages are getting through?

22

WHY A PURPOSE-DRIVEN LIFE IN BUSINESS PAYS OFF

After years building a successful career as an investment banker at William Blair, I realized it was time to step back a bit from work and do something intellectually stimulating, yet a little less intensive in terms of travel and time away from my family.

As I considered what that move might be, an opportunity emerged to join my alma mater as a finance professor and the leader of an organization called the Investment Banking Academy. The IBA prepares students for investment banking and private equity careers, so the opportunity was naturally appealing.

Fortunately, that career change turned out to be one of the most rewarding things I've ever done. Teaching a new generation of business leaders at one of the nation's top business programs has also taught me a lot about leadership and working with a true sense of purpose, no matter what career path you choose.

I attribute some of those leadership lessons to Larry Gies, a former classmate of mine at Illinois.

A few years after I arrived at Illinois in 2015, I had the incredible opportunity to connect Larry with Jeff Brown, the new dean of our business school. Larry and I had maintained a friendship after college, and I had watched him quietly build an amazing career. The company he founded not long after we graduated, Madison Industries, is now among the largest privately-held companies in the US. At that first meeting, Larry and Jeff discussed Jeff's vision for the college and his views on high-quality public education. Given the kind of groundbreaking and purpose-driven leader that Larry is, I shouldn't have been surprised that Larry soon decided to give Illinois' College of Business an astounding gift of $150 million, one of the largest gifts ever awarded by a single donor to a college of business.

In addition to being a charismatic leader, Larry is also an extremely humble guy. He initially resisted having the school named after him, but the dean convinced him that naming the school would be even more impactful in enhancing the school's visibility and elevating its strong reputation into an even more powerful one around the country. Larry also importantly embraced the brand promise of the newly named Gies College of Business:

"BUSINESS ON PURPOSE."

This is about preparing our students to approach business differently, with the goal of making a difference. College leaders aim to instill in students the notion that through business, they can not only build a successful life for their families, but also have a positive impact on society. For all our students, including many first-generation college-goers, the message truly resonates.

For those of us on faculty at the time, delivering "Business on Purpose" would be accomplished through intentional actions—delivering insights in the classroom, offering unique programs with motivational alumni, and introducing experiential learning courses with leaders at top employers.

This approach definitely stretched the boundaries of what was considered a traditional business education, yet there was a commitment among the faculty and the professional staff to make the Gies education well-rounded, unique, and meaningful.

Larry did his part by staying regularly engaged, visiting campus, guest lecturing, and getting to know many students on a personal level. In a way, he was demonstrating his own master class in purposeful leadership, and it inspired many of us.

CONTINUED...

Importantly, his leadership also helped create an environment that encouraged creativity and enabled new perspectives. While teaching the core theories of finance, accounting, and marketing was still essential, expanding the boundaries of what business education delivered was equally critical in developing the next generation of business leaders.

My personal call to action was about assessing what my unique personal assets were and how I could leverage them into creating a second-to-none learning opportunity for our students.

I reflected on my 30-year career, during which I had assembled a wide professional network of leaders in finance, private equity, and venture capital. I enjoyed engaging with them in a personal way that created mutually beneficial outcomes in an academic setting. I decided part of my purpose was to continue making connections with business and academic leaders and working with them to create incredibly positive outcomes—for themselves and for those around them.

This call to action has resulted in the introduction of three classes which have been well received by our students. The first involved an in-class internship for seniors in finance, pairing them with top-tier private equity and venture capital firms across the country. This experiential learning class is one of the largest of its kind at the undergraduate level, allowing students to experience firsthand what it means to be a private equity professional. Importantly, it creates a win-win, as the employers obtain valuable input from a motivated group of senior finance students as well.

The second class I created (in concert with other professional academics) is the Golder Freshman Seminar, a course exposing freshmen to 12 career panels during their first semester. Ranging from topics like investment banking, commercial banking, private equity, investment management, and real estate, this class allows younger students to learn about careers from young professionals at a formative time.

The last class I created involved a book written by James Kerr, entitled *Legacy*. The book features leadership lessons from the New Zealand All Blacks rugby team, generally considered the most successful sporting franchise in history. In this class, I partnered with several of our most inspirational alumni. Each chose a leadership principle from the book and taught a class that personalized it to their own career experience. I've loved the stories coming out of those sessions. It's exciting to see students learn from amazing leaders at a critical time in their own leadership journey. What's most rewarding from my personal work and those of my colleagues is that many of the goals we've set are being achieved. Illinois is now rated as a top-five public undergraduate business school, a meaningful improvement from where we were when the Gies naming took place. While all of this has been great for the academic environment at Illinois and the Gies College of Business, the parallels to the business world are strong and clear. When leaders set an inspiring mission, ensure that everyone is bought in, and create an environment that encourages each person to put their own unique touch on its delivery, the results for the organization are game-changing.

> For me, "Business on Purpose" is so much more than a mission. It is what makes any leader—and this business school—truly great.

ROB METZGER

CLINICAL PROFESSOR OF FINANCE, GIES COLLEGE OF BUSINESS AT THE UNIVERSITY OF ILLINOIS URBANA-CHAMPAIGN

MAKING CAREER TRANSITIONS WORK: A LEADER'S GUIDE TO SUPPORTING GROWTH

Career changes come in many forms. Sometimes, it's growing into a new role while staying with the same leader and team. Other times, it means moving to a new department with different leadership. Both scenarios represent significant personal transitions.

As current or future leaders of these employees, our role is to help them see these changes as growth opportunities while ensuring they feel supported through the journey—whether we're helping them grow within our team or preparing them for success elsewhere in the organization.

Here are some of the most common questions I hear from leaders about managing career transitions:

Q: Why do employees hesitate to pursue new opportunities even when they're clearly ready?

A: Les Landes, a colleague of mine, shares a powerful insight: "It's not that people resist change. People resist being changed." When employees feel pushed into a new role or career direction without input, resistance naturally follows. This is true whether they're considering a new role on their current team or a move to a different department. The key is helping them explore opportunities and make informed choices about their growth path while assuring them that you'll support their development—even if that means eventually losing them to another team.

Q: What's the importance of a development plan for every employee and regular developmental discussions?

A: Development plans provide both direction and accountability for growth. When every employee has a clear plan, they understand exactly what skills they need to develop, what experiences would benefit them, and what success looks like. Regular discussions about these plans—monthly at minimum—keep development active rather than something that's only discussed during annual reviews. These conversations also help you identify when someone's ready for new challenges before they become restless or look elsewhere for growth.

Q: When should we start discussing career changes with employees?

A: Earlier than you might think. Start by exploring possibilities—discuss aspirations, potential paths, and concerns openly. Then, create a development plan and maintain regular check-ins. Finally, evaluate progress as you go, celebrating early wins and adjusting support based on what you learn.

Leader Self-Check Questions

Before your next career development conversation, ask yourself:

1. How am I helping employees explore growth opportunities?

2. What support systems do I have in place for transitions?

3. How am I recognizing progress and celebrating growth?

4. Where might fears or concerns exist, and how can I address them?

5. What's my plan for ongoing development support?

REMEMBER:

Career transitions aren't something that happen to your team—they're opportunities you explore together. When employees feel supported in their growth journey, they're more likely to take positive steps forward.

BUILDING A GROWTH-CONNECTED ORGANIZATION:

A GUIDE FOR SENIOR LEADERSHIP TEAMS

As a senior leadership team, your collective approach to connecting strategy with employee growth creates a multiplier effect that transforms both culture and results. When employees clearly see how their development aligns with organizational strategy, engagement soars and performance accelerates. Here are the key actions your leadership team can take to make strategy-connected growth your competitive advantage:

1 Align on Employee Development as a Strategic Priority

Why This Matters: Senior teams that treat employee development as a strategic imperative see significantly higher levels of engagement and performance.

Leadership Team Actions:

- Include development metrics in your organizational dashboard
- Make career growth a standing agenda item in leadership meetings
- Ensure regular succession planning discussions
- Share employee development success stories in company communications
- Connect individual growth directly to business outcomes
- Measure and track the impact of development initiatives

2 Create Systematic Employee Development Touchpoints

Why This Matters: When development becomes systematic, it becomes sustainable. Build growth conversations into your existing business rhythms.

Leadership Team Actions:

- Start every executive meeting with development progress updates
- Create monthly talent review roundtables
- Establish quarterly career check-ins
- Design annual development celebrations
- Build growth planning into your strategic planning process

3 Model Cross-Functional Development

Why This Matters: Breaking down silos starts with leaders actively supporting development across departmental lines.

Leadership Team Actions:

- Share talent across departments for growth
- Build mentorship programs across functions
- Celebrate collaborative development wins
- Document and share cross-team success stories

CONTINUED

BUILDING A GROWTH-CONNECTED ORGANIZATION:

A GUIDE FOR SENIOR LEADERSHIP TEAMS

4 Develop Your Organization's Employee Development Capability

Why This Matters: Building a development-focused culture requires strengthening leadership capability at all levels.

Leadership Team Actions:

- Invest in leadership development at all levels
- Create career conversation toolkits for managers
- Establish mentoring programs focused on growth
- Share best practices across divisions
- Measure and reward effective development practices

5 Build Employee Development Into Your Talent Systems

Why This Matters: Embedding development into your talent processes ensures it becomes part of how you operate, not just what you say.

Leadership Team Actions:

- Include development skills in leadership competencies
- Evaluate growth effectiveness in performance reviews
- Consider development practices in promotion decisions
- Build career planning into onboarding programs
- Reward managers who excel at developing talent

6 Create Accountability for Employee Development

Why This Matters: What gets measured gets done. Create clear expectations and accountability for development.

Leadership Team Actions:

- Set specific development goals for each leader
- Track career progression patterns and frequency
- Measure the impact on employee engagement
- Include development metrics in business reviews
- Share growth analytics across the organization

QUESTIONS FOR YOUR NEXT SENIOR TEAM MEETING

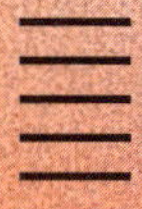

1. How effectively are we modeling employee development-focused leadership as a team?
2. Where are the gaps in our current development practices?
3. What systems could we create to make career growth more consistent?
4. How are we measuring the impact of our development practices?
5. What's one thing we could do differently starting tomorrow?

ACCESS POPULAR STRATEGY ACTIVATION RESOURCES

FREE

7 EMPLOYEE GROWTH & DEVELOPMENT IDEAS FOR LEADERS

Blog

PAINT A PICTURE OF THE FUTURE

MAXIMIZING STRATEGY DEVELOPMENT & ROLLOUT WITH TOP LEADERS

eBook

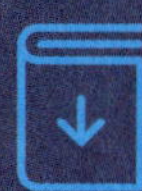

HOW TO ACTIVATE & EMBED YOUR STRATEGY TO ACCELERATE RESULTS

eBook

6. ENABLE EMPLOYEES TO MEET THE MOMENT

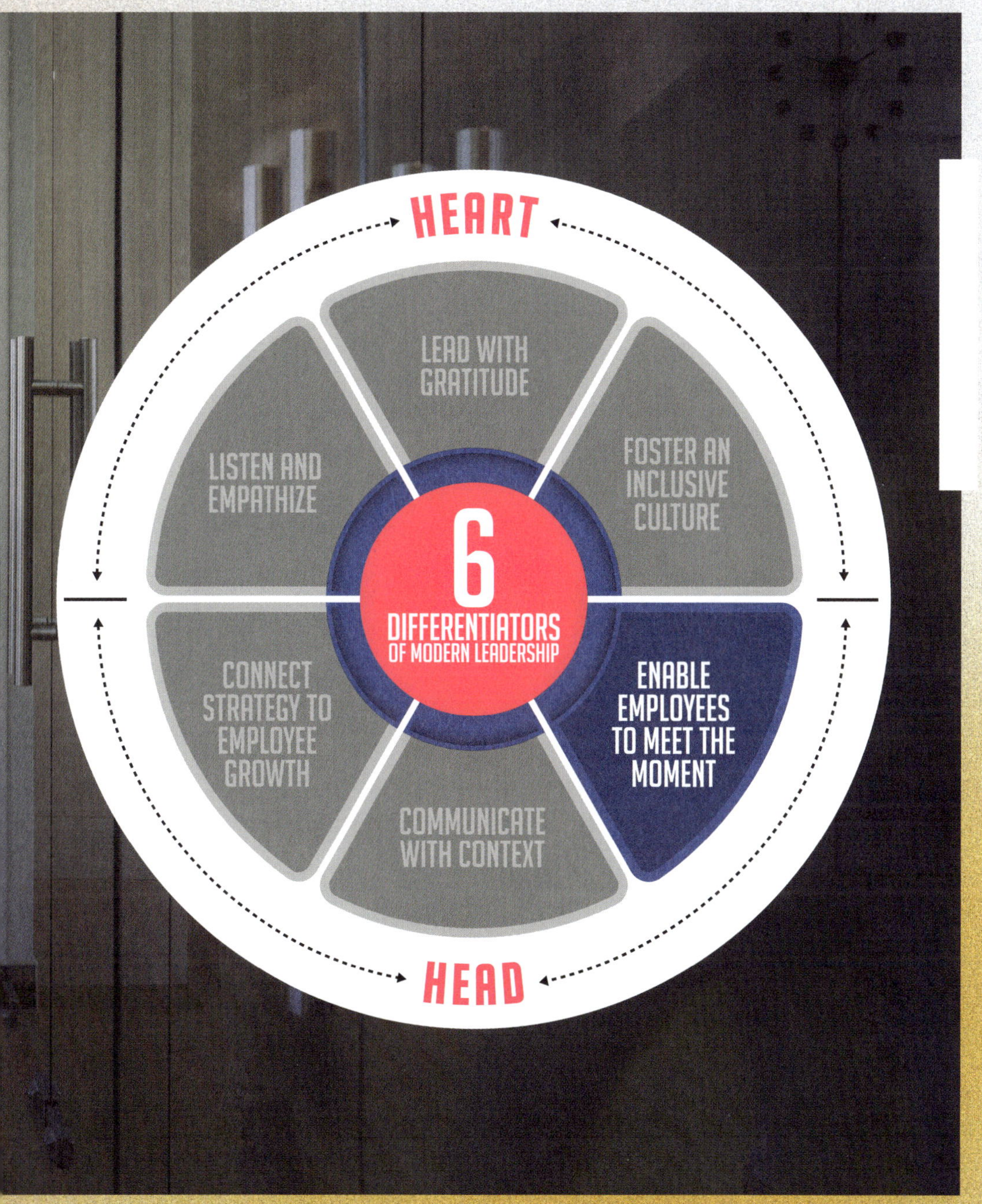
HEART
LEAD WITH GRATITUDE
FOSTER AN INCLUSIVE CULTURE
LISTEN AND EMPATHIZE
6
DIFFERENTIATORS
OF MODERN LEADERSHIP
CONNECT STRATEGY TO EMPLOYEE GROWTH
ENABLE EMPLOYEES TO MEET THE MOMENT
COMMUNICATE WITH CONTEXT
HEAD

Picture two different leadership scenarios. In one, a leader spends their days assigning tasks, monitoring progress, and stepping in to solve problems. In another, a leader creates the conditions where employees naturally step up, collaborate, and innovate to drive results. Which scenario matches your current approach? And more importantly, which approach do you think leads to sustained success?

AS LEADERS, WE FACE A PIVOTAL QUESTION:

HOW DO WE ENABLE OUR EMPLOYEES TO MEET THIS MOMENT?

I recently spoke with Robert, a senior executive at a Fortune 500 company, who shared a telling story. "For years," he said, "I thought my role was to simply set clear expectations and then get out of the way. But in today's environment, that's not enough. Employees need more than direction—they need enablement, connection, and purpose." Robert's insight cuts to the heart of Modern Leadership. The most successful leaders today don't manage—they enable.

THEY UNDERSTAND THAT THEIR ROLE IS TO:

Understand the work that needs to be done and match it with the right talent

Foster meaningful collaboration that drives innovation and performance

Connect employees to best practices and outside perspectives that spark growth

Help everyone see how their individual contributions ladder up to organizational purpose

Deploy technology in ways that enhance both productivity and culture

The pace of change in today's business environment means that traditional management approaches no longer suffice. Leaders must evolve from simply directing work to enabling their people to succeed. This requires a fundamental shift in how we think about leadership. As one CEO recently told me, "The difference between good and great organizations today isn't strategy or execution—it's how well leaders enable their people to bring their best selves to work every day."

Throughout this chapter, we'll explore practical strategies for making this shift. You'll discover proven approaches, learn specific techniques you can implement immediately, and gain insights on creating an environment where employees don't simply survive—they thrive.

WHAT THE RESEARCH SAYS

Less than half

OF EMPLOYEES ***(47%)*** SAY THEIR MANAGER UNDERSTANDS THEIR CURRENT SKILLS, INTERESTS, AND SKILL GAPS.[1]

COMPANIES FAIL TO CHOOSE THE RIGHT CANDIDATE FOR MANAGERIAL POSITIONS

of the time.[2]

SOURCE

[1]Bravery, K. et al, (2024) 2024 Global Talent Trends. Mercer Global Trends 2024.

[2]Harter, J. (March, 2014) Why great managers are rare. Gallup.

Employees who experience high role clarity are 53% more efficient AND ***27% MORE EFFECTIVE*** AT WORK COMPARED TO THOSE EXPERIENCING ROLE AMBIGUITY.[3]

IMPROVING COLLABORATION IN THE WORKPLACE COULD LEAD TO A GAIN OF **$2,517 per employee annually.**[4]

[3]Pijnacker, L. (2019). HR Analytics: Role Clarity Impacts Performance. Effectory.

[4]Deloitte Access Economics (2014) The Collaborative Economy. Deloitte Access Economics.

23

LEADERSHIP IS ABOUT SETTING THE TONE

I will never forget my first month on the job as a People and Culture leader at a previous organization. The industry was hit with an unexpected regulatory change, one that we all knew would have a negative impact on our company. When we learned of this massive change, there was a definite feeling of frustration and uncertainty.

Yet, thanks to the CEO of our organization at the time, that feeling didn't last long. As we gathered in the boardroom to discuss the news, our CEO simply said, "I'm giving you all a few minutes to just absorb this and share your frustrations. But then we need to stop, focus on solutions, and walk out to our teams with a sense of calm and confidence. We need to tell them we're going to be OK. We're going to figure it out, and we're going to work together to get through this."

That was such a pivotal leadership moment for me, and since then, I have worked to model this former CEO's style in all my subsequent leadership roles. I often use the phrase, "Take in the heat and radiate calm," words I learned from a great former leader. I believe leaders have a responsibility to guide their teams through change with confidence and resolve, helping employees stay solution-focused and unlock their potential. Strong leaders should model the culture they want to create.

Time and again, I have seen leaders succeed when they take time to set the right tone—in their communication, in their interactions with employees and customers, and in their decision-making. Leaders need to show their teams that they consider feedback and input while not shying away from the tough moments. As businesses continuously pivot and adjust to various internal and external factors, leaders must be flexible and humble enough to try something different when needed.

At my current company, CareRx, I've seen how essential leadership style is in driving success, complementing the data-driven decisions we make. Having leaders who build genuine relationships with their team members, listen to their needs, and respond accordingly makes a huge difference in retention. We know this because we track retention monthly by pharmacy, and we see this in the data. When managers known for coaching and bringing out the best in their employees are brought in, the results are clear: retention improves, employees feel supported, and engagement goes up.

Leaders need to demonstrate authentic concern for what matters to employees, not just what matters to the bottom line. Our current CEO, Puneet Khanna, does this exceptionally well. When we introduced large-scale changes to improve processes in our pharmacies, his first guiding principle was: "We want every employee to get home in time to have dinner with their family."

This simple statement says so much about what matters; it's not just "what" we do, but "how" we do it. We continue to focus on both the customer and employee experience, believing that this relationship is intertwined. When employees can be productive and do their best work, they're naturally able to better serve our customers. That's always a win-win for the business. In fact, our senior leaders feel so strongly about a positive customer experience, both internally and externally, that we now provide mandatory customer service training for all our employees.

Another way we have enabled our teams to improve the employee and customer experience is by introducing short, daily huddles in our pharmacies to review our goals and progress. We celebrate wins and focus on key learnings for future improvement. What I love most about this process is that employees have the chance to bring forward questions, comments, and suggestions.

It's incredibly exciting to hear employees cheering during team huddles when they meet or exceed their goals. With such clear expectations, there's built-in accountability, transparency, and pride. This pride also starts with our leaders—and that's the kind of culture I'm proud to be a part of.

ADRIANNE SULLIVAN-CAMPEAU

CHIEF EMPLOYEE & CUSTOMER EXPERIENCE OFFICER, CARERX CORPORATION, CANADA

DECODING THE "NOW": WHAT EMPLOYEES REALLY NEED TO THRIVE

Imagine your team not just working, but truly coming alive. The workplace isn't simply changing—it's being reinvented in real time. Employees today are seeking more than a job; they're looking for a meaningful journey that connects their individual potential with something larger than themselves.

The Heart of the Matter

Employees are telling us something profound: They want to be seen, heard, and empowered. This isn't about perks or ping-pong tables—it's about creating an environment where human potential can flourish.

Five Critical Insights Leaders Must Understand

1. Technology as a Human Amplifier: Forget viewing technology as a threat. The most successful leaders see digital tools as superpowers that can unlock creativity, learning, and human potential. How can you transform technological change from a challenge into an opportunity for growth?

2. Flexibility Is the New Currency: For many, work is no longer a place you go—it's something you do. Employees are seeking employers who understand that life doesn't fit neatly into a 9-to-5 box. Flexibility isn't a perk; it demonstrates fundamental respect for individual needs. Where and when possible, every individual needs a personalized solution.

3. Purpose Over Paycheck: Today's workforce wants to know their work matters. They're asking: "How does my daily effort contribute to something meaningful?" Leaders and employees who can clearly articulate this connection create unprecedented levels of engagement. (But the paycheck still matters, too.)

4. Psychological Safety Matters: Creating an environment where employees feel safe to speak up, take risks, and be themselves isn't soft—it's strategic. Psychological safety is the foundation of innovation, collaboration, and high performance.

5. Continuous Learning as a Lifeline: The half-life of skills is shrinking. Employees need organizations committed to continuous learning, where professional development isn't an annual checkbox, but a daily commitment.

Reflection Questions

- When was the last time you listened for your team's unspoken needs?
- How might your current leadership approach be unintentionally creating barriers?
- Are you viewing your employees as resources to be managed, or as partners to be inspired?

REMEMBER:

Take 15 minutes to have an honest conversation with yourself. Map out the invisible barriers in your current workplace culture. What small, meaningful changes could you implement today that signal genuine care and commitment to your team's holistic success?

WALL OR CASTLE: HELPING EMPLOYEES KNOW HOW THEY FIT IN

There were two bricklayers, both performing the same task. When asked what they're doing, one responds, "I'm building a wall." The other says, "I'm building a castle." Same job, but dramatically different perspectives.
In today's workplace, it's easy to get lost in the day-to-day grind. But here's the truth: Employees crave more than completing tasks. They want to understand how their work matters—how they're not solely laying bricks, but creating something extraordinary.

Understanding Your Wall and Your Castle

Employees needs to articulate two things:

1. **What They Do (The Wall):** A tactical description of their role. For example: "I work at corporate and am developing an app for farmers."
2. **How They Contribute (The Castle):** The meaningful impact behind their work. Continuing our example: "What I'm really doing is helping farmers increase their crop yield, sustaining their business, feeding more people, and supporting global food security."

Consider these additional examples:

- "I process payroll reports" vs. "I ensure our employees can provide for their families"
- "I write code" vs. "I'm making technology accessible to everyone"
- "I answer customer calls" vs. "I help people solve problems that matter to them"

The difference isn't semantic—it's transformative. When people understand their "castle," they bring more energy, creativity, and commitment to their work.

The Castle-Building Exercise: A Powerful Team Activity

Ready to transform your team's perspective? Here's a six-step approach to help employees articulate their unique contributions:

1. Challenge Employees' Thinking: Encourage team members to explore how their work connects to broader organizational goals.

2. Explain the Why: Help them understand that this exercise isn't simply an activity—it's about recognizing each person's genuine value.

3. Lead by Example: Share your own understanding of how your role contributes to the larger mission. Vulnerability breeds connection.

4. Encourage Personal Reflection: Ask employees to write down their thoughts. Remind them there are no "right" or "wrong" answers.

5. Create a Sharing Moment: Have each team member share their insights. Pro tip: Promise (and deliver) enthusiastic applause!

6. Gather Collective Wisdom: After sharing, discuss what worked well and how the team can further clarify their collective purpose.

What You Might Discover

This exercise often reveals surprising insights:

- Employees may not fully understand the organization's strategy
- Team priorities might need clarification
- Individual roles can be better aligned with organizational goals

Common Pitfalls to Avoid

1. Over-Inflating Impact: Be honest and realistic about contributions while still acknowledging their importance

2. One-Size-Fits-All Messaging: Different employees may find meaning in different aspects of their work

3. Set-and-Forget Communication: Connection to purpose needs regular reinforcement and discussion

Reflection Questions

- How well can your team members articulate the "castle" they're building, beyond their daily tasks?
- Can you clearly describe how your own role contributes to the organization's larger mission?
- Are there team members who seem disconnected or "building a wall"? How might you reignite their sense of purpose?
- What small, consistent steps can you take to regularly reinforce the importance of each team member's unique contribution?

REMEMBER:
When employees see their castle, they bring their best selves to work. More importantly, they become architects of something greater than themselves—and that's what exceptional leadership is all about.

5 WAYS TO ENCOURAGE COLLABORATION

Think about the last great project you were part of. Chances are, its success wasn't solely about individual contributions—it was about how well the team worked together. Yet, many leaders struggle with a fundamental paradox: How do you encourage organic collaboration without forcing it? How do you create an environment where teamwork flourishes naturally?

Here are five proven approaches that can transform your team's culture:

1. Create Purposeful Connections

Don't throw people together and expect magic to happen. Instead:

- Match people with complementary skills and perspectives
- Be clear about why collaboration matters for specific projects
- Help team members understand each other's strengths
- Create a team charter to clarify direction and how to work together
- Create opportunities for informal connections beyond formal meetings

Quick Win: Start team meetings by having members share their unique superpower related to the current project.

2. Design for Collaboration

Your physical and virtual workspace significantly impacts how people work together:

- Ensure technology tools support rather than hinder connection
- Create both formal and informal spaces for collaboration
- Remove unnecessary barriers between teams and departments
- Consider how hybrid work arrangements affect collaboration patterns

Quick Win: Audit your current collaboration tools. Are they helping or creating friction? Ask your team what would make working together easier.

3. Model Collaborative Behavior

Your actions as a leader set the tone:

- Actively seek input from others
- Share credit generously
- Admit when you need help
- Make your thinking visible to others
- Show appreciation for collaborative efforts

Quick Win: In your next meeting, explicitly share how input from others improved your thinking on a particular issue.

4. Build Trust Through Transparency

Collaboration flourishes in high-trust environments:

- Share context and information openly
- Be clear about decision-making processes
- Address conflicts directly and constructively
- Create psychological safety for taking risks
- Follow through on commitments

Quick Win: Create clear "rules of engagement" with your team about how you'll work together and make decisions.

5. Reward and Recognize Collaborative Success

What gets recognized gets repeated:

- Celebrate team wins, not solely individual achievements
- Share stories of successful collaboration
- Include collaboration in performance discussions
- Create opportunities for teams to reflect on what's working

Quick Win: Start your next team meeting by highlighting a recent example of great collaboration and its impact.

YOUR NEXT STEPS

1

For Leaders:

- Which of these five areas needs the most attention in your team?
- What's one small step you could take this week in each area?
- How will you know if your efforts are working?

2

For Your Team:

- What barriers to collaboration currently exist?
- What would make it easier to work together effectively?
- What does successful collaboration look like to them?

REMEMBER:

True collaboration isn't about forcing people to work together—it's about creating conditions where working together is the natural and rewarding choice. Start small, be consistent, and celebrate progress along the way.

24

HOW YOU HANDLE DEFEAT DEFINES FUTURE SUCCESS

When you work in the pharmaceutical industry, everything you do is centered on how you can improve the lives of those you serve. Yes, we worry about the length of patents and revenue streams and profit margins, but what drives you to work all weekend or late into the night on a continual basis are the conversations you have had with people battling disease who are counting on you to get new drugs to market. It's personal.

One of the world's most successful drugs to treat cancer, Taxotere (docetaxel), was discovered in the mid-1980s by ICSN (Institut de Chimie des Substances Naturelles) researchers led by Paris-based Pierre Potier, who figured out how to synthesize Taxotere from the English yew (Taxus baccata). From here, the journey begins with a patent in 1986, followed by a drug development process that studied the safety of this potential treatment, followed by Phase I and II clinical trials to prepare for a submission to regulatory authorities. Rhone-Poulenc Rorer (now Sanofi) created a team that dedicated significant resources to develop this important drug. For all of us working on Taxotere, we realized how important it could be to thousands, if not millions, of people battling cancer.

Finally, we were ready to visit the US Food and Drug Administration and present to the Oncologic Drugs Advisory Committee (ODAC) on December 14, 1994. We knew our team was presenting a very important and highly active chemotherapy treatment. All of the late nights, missed family events, and continual travel were going to be worth it. We were excited. Until the vote.

ODAC voted 6-0 with two abstentions to reject Taxotere for the treatment of advanced breast cancer. We were devastated. Shocked. Confused. Immediately, Rob Cawthorn and Michel de Rosen, the Chair and CEO of Rhone-Poulenc Rorer, summoned us to return from D.C. and meet in the boardroom of our company in Collegeville, Pennsylvania. As we walked into the boardroom, we expected a meeting to analyze our faults, but that was not to happen. The meeting centered, rather quickly, on what we would do to ensure this important treatment received approval in the future. We were instructed to work full speed and let nothing get in our way to achieve our goal. We were encouraged in side conversations to lead in our respective areas and move with speed. Within the same day, we went from being distraught to being inspired and completely focused on our new goal. Right at the center of this thinking was a belief that the people battling cancer were the ones who mattered, not us. It was our obligation and duty to ensure they were able to access a treatment with therapeutic potential. This one meeting set the tone for the years ahead. We knew our leaders had our backs. We knew our leaders believed in us and would open any door we could only partially pry open. And they reminded us how urgent it was to succeed. Days mattered.

Fast forward and our team returned to ODAC on May 15, 1996, where we received a conditional (and unanimous) approval for treatment of locally advanced or metastatic breast cancer. Full approval was granted in 1998, and new indications to treat different types of cancer were added in the years following. In 2010, Sanofi, now the leader for Taxotere, reported that more than 1.5 million people were treated and annual sales were $3.1 billion. Taxotere had become one of the more important cancer drugs to reach the market in its history. We believed this was possible in 1994. With different leaders at the helm, the drug may not have made it to market. Or the company might have sold the drug rights to another company, further delaying its approval, or perhaps a merger could have deprioritized it. It would have been easy to fail or pivot or deflect. Instead, our leaders became more resolute, more focused, and relentless in achieving our vision. And so did we. When we walked out of that boardroom on a gloomy December evening in 1994, we knew it was our job to define our future.

We could have given up and spent time lamenting. But we didn't. We became more determined. And we were more determined because, to us, 1.5 million people is not an abstract number. It was a reflection of the hundreds of conversations we were having with people battling cancer who were counting on us. We felt their burden, turned it into our energy, and the rest is history. That is what a successful attitude looks and feels like. It is real, long-term, and it treats issues as speed bumps on the road to success.

Thank you to Rob Cawthorn, Michel de Rosen, and the many leaders who made it all happen. It was a moment in my life that I rely on to motivate me when I need an extra push. Making a difference in our world is never about ourselves. It is always about who benefits from our work.

BEYOND INSULAR: HOW TO BRING IN OUTSIDE PERSPECTIVES

Imagine your organization as a greenhouse. Without fresh air, sunlight, and occasional cross-pollination, even the most promising seeds will struggle to grow. The same is true for your team's potential.

In today's rapidly evolving business landscape, insularity is the silent killer of innovation. Leaders who default to internal echo chambers are unknowingly limiting their team's capacity to thrive, adapt, and break through.

Why Outside Perspectives Matter

Let's be clear: Your team's greatest asset isn't the talent within your walls—it's their ability to continuously learn, challenge assumptions, and see beyond their immediate environment. Outside perspectives aren't a luxury; they're a strategic imperative.

The Three Critical Lenses of External Insight

1. Disruption Awareness: Breakthrough ideas rarely emerge from comfortable spaces. By intentionally exposing your team to external thinking, you create a culture of curiosity. This isn't about wholesale change; it's about expanding your team's peripheral vision. When employees are exposed to ideas from different industries, diverse thought leaders, and emerging trends, they develop "adaptive intelligence"—the ability to see opportunities where others see obstacles.

2. Psychological Safety in Learning: Bringing in outside perspectives requires creating an environment where your team feels safe exploring new ideas without fear of judgment. It's about saying, "We don't have all the answers, and that's exciting." When leaders model intellectual humility, teams become more open, resilient, and innovative.

3. Continuous Growth Mindset: Outside perspectives transform learning from a checkbox activity to a living, breathing culture. It's not about attending an occasional conference—it's about making external exploration and insights a consistent part of your organizational DNA.

Practical Strategies for Bringing in Outside Perspectives

1. Curate Intentional Learning Experiences

Create a "Perspective Passport" that encourages team members to:

- Attend cross-industry conferences
- Participate in external workshops
- Connect with thought leaders beyond your immediate domain

2. Build Structured External Engagement

Develop formal mechanisms for fresh insights:

- Host quarterly guest speaker series
- Create cross-industry advisory panels
- Establish mentorship opportunities with external experts

3. Break Down Internal Barriers

Challenge traditional thinking by:

- Rotating team members across departments
- Creating cross-functional innovation teams
- Hosting inter-departmental idea exchanges

4. Leverage Technology as a Learning Accelerator

Use digital platforms to:

- Provide curated industry insights
- Enable global knowledge exchanges
- Connect your team with diverse thought communities

REMEMBER:

Bringing in outside perspectives isn't a top-down mandate. It's a cultural invitation. Leaders who succeed don't direct—they inspire a genuine hunger for learning.

The future belongs to those brave enough to look beyond their current horizons.

You can make it happen.

25

WHAT IT REALLY TAKES TO BE A BETTER LEADER TODAY

For many years, I've worked as an executive coach for business owners and senior executives. What's fascinating is how much the first half of my career—20 years as a psychotherapist—prepared me for a pivot to supporting leaders in being the best they can be.

While my business clients tend to have stronger support systems overall, I've realized the two client groups are also alike in many ways. Both are overworked, overstressed, lonely, self-critical, and exhausted, physically and emotionally. The top industry leaders whom I'm proud to support often exude strong exteriors, yet they can confront intense interior challenges that are much the same as everyone else's.

However, it's exciting and encouraging to me that the opportunities for real change and growth—for both groups—are tremendous. The key often comes down to the ability of leaders to look inside themselves and honestly assess what they are doing well and what they could still improve to create a culture people truly want to be part of.

Self-assessment and an openness to change and growth are easy to embrace in concept but require attention and focus to actually achieve. Still, when leaders make that commitment, that's where greatness lies, for both the leaders themselves and the teams that they lead.

There are naturally many sides to this important leadership work, but I've found three aspects particularly helpful, highlighted here through stories from my personal experience:

1 GET VERY GOOD AT PRIORITIZING WHAT'S IMPORTANT.

A key piece of leading for success is limiting the sheer number of priorities you set for your team. Sometimes, the most energetic and creative leaders are terrible at this. One example is a leader I worked with named Saul (I've changed names for some stories here to protect client privacy). Saul was an avid reader and an innovative thinker, and he loved trying out new approaches. It felt as if he had a breakthrough idea he wanted to share weekly, and he often held meetings to launch employee groups in exploring the concepts. That was all fine except for one thing; Saul never remembered to follow up with his team members to say:

"YOU KNOW THAT JUMPING BEAN INITIATIVE WE STARTED ON LAST MONTH? I'M KILLING IT OFF—IT'S NOT THE WAY WE'RE GOING TO GO."

He just kept piling more and more on. To be fair, Saul's team loved him—he was an exciting leader to work for—and they prided themselves on their ability to keep up with him. But racing toward new ideas without eliminating some old ones was starting to burn his team out. Fortunately, he realized this and began to hold "Liberation Parties," where projects were killed off.

As a result, his team became more productive than ever. What helped Saul through this personal challenge was his willingness to accept feedback that the idea avalanche was actually hurting the business and team morale, and he was courageous enough to self-correct.

CONTINUED...

2 TAKE EMPATHY TO THE NEXT LEVEL.

A big theme of mine is the ability of leaders to "curate" their work and personal lives, knowing there's a finite amount of tasks any one human can accomplish in a day's work, no matter how talented he or she may be. Great leaders know how to not just talk about managing one's personal energy but also how to model that behavior and reward it.

In many high-stress, high-demand roles, it may not be enough to verbally limit your demands on employees. Occasionally, leaders need to intervene in the demands employees set for themselves. My favorite story about this kind of leadership comes from my father's history. My father, Walter Hartmann, escaped Nazi Germany in 1939 on the Kindertransport, the remarkable humanitarian initiative by Great Britain to help move Jewish children out of Germany and into England.

My father then lived through World War II in England, working a variety of jobs, and wanted to give back somehow. He found that chance through a rehabilitation center serving youths who had been liberated from the concentration camps after the war. Working at one of the centers, Windermere, my father saw many children who had been shattered by the losses and horrors they witnessed, so much so that he later became a psychologist. However, at that time, he had no training for the work he needed to do. As a Holocaust survivor himself, he had lost both parents to the genocide, and the work undoubtedly triggered his own traumas.

However, the leader of Windermere understood this and established a surprising policy for people like my father. On the one day per week that the staff had off, staff members were not permitted to be at the center. They weren't just encouraged to take a break; they were required to. The leader knew that the staff was so committed to the children that they would work themselves into the ground unless he prevented it.

Fortunately, very few people have jobs as emotionally devastating as those serving in this camp. Nonetheless, many people invest a lot of emotional energy in their work, and sometimes it is the job of the leader to insist that employees observe boundaries that they otherwise might ignore. Part of a manager's job is to help create an environment that enables his or her team to do their best work, and sometimes that means telling them to go home. In doing so, leaders earn genuine trust and respect from their employees because employees feel seen, respected, and recognized for the impact they have.

3 SHOW GRATITUDE.

I worked for some years as a clinical psychologist in a medical center. The medical director was a renowned physician, a tall, brilliant Scot whom we all admired immensely. Dr. McSherry was a very busy leader with a broad scope of responsibility. Yet every once in a while when I was giving a presentation to the medical residents, I would see him standing at the back of the room, listening.

Sometimes, within a day or two, I'd get a handwritten note from Dr. McSherry praising my work. Those notes meant the world to me. Dr. McSherry didn't send them all the time, just when he thought something was outstanding. They inspired me to do my best and affirmed that I was doing great work.

It's been 20 years since I left the medical center and Dr. McSherry has passed away, but I still have those notes.

Gratitude is discussed a lot more in leadership circles today, yet sometimes it's still considered a "nice-to-have." I believe it's more essential than ever toward building an exceptional rapport with employees.

In all of my work, I've seen how much outstanding leadership relies on a drive to make meaningful connections with employees. It's about listening more intently, recognizing the value that each person brings to their specific role, and respecting the boundaries we all face in the time and energy we can realistically devote to making positive change.

GAIL GOLDEN

PRINCIPAL,
GAIL GOLDEN
CONSULTING

DEPLOYING TECHNOLOGY THAT MATTERS

Q: Why is technology deployment a critical leadership challenge today?

A: Technology isn't simply about tools—it's about human potential. In today's rapidly changing workplace, leaders face a pivotal choice: Will technology be a barrier or a bridge? The most successful organizations view technology as a way to unlock their team's creativity, not replace human insight.

Q: What are the biggest mistakes leaders make when introducing new technology?

A: Three critical pitfalls emerge:

1. Falling in Love with Features, Not People: Leaders often get dazzled by shiny tech solutions without understanding their team's real needs. True transformation starts with listening, not buying.

2. Ignoring the Human Experience: Technology should reduce friction, not create it. If your new system makes employees' work more complicated, you've missed the point entirely.

3. Treating Technology as a Transaction, Not a Transformation: Successful technology deployment is a journey of cultural change, not a purchasing decision.

Q: How can leaders ensure technology actually improves workload and culture?

A: Think of technology as a collaborative partner, not a replacement. Key strategies include:

- **Listen Deeply:** Before any implementation, have genuine conversations with your team.
- **Connect to Purpose:** Choose technologies that directly support your organization's mission.
- **Prioritize Learning:** Create robust training and support mechanisms.
- **Stay Flexible:** View technology deployment as an ongoing dialogue, not a one-time event.

Q: What questions should leaders ask before deploying new technology?

A: Critical reflection questions include:

- Will this technology genuinely make us smarter and more efficient?
- How does this align with our core values?
- What skills do we need to develop?
- How will we measure both operational and cultural impact?

REMEMBER:

Technology is most powerful when it becomes invisible—when it simply helps people do what they do best.

Q: What's the human element in technological transformation?

A: Technology should be a bridge, not a barrier. The most powerful technological solutions:

- Reduce unnecessary friction
- Create space for human creativity
- Demonstrate genuine care for employee experience
- Enable rather than restrict

26

"EVERYONE CAN MAKE MISTAKES HERE. THE KEY IS MAKING THEM ONLY ONCE."

I was fortunate to start my career working for two PR agency glass-ceiling breakers, Jean Way Schoonover and her sister Barbara Hunter, at Dudley-Anderson-Yutzy (DAY) Public Relations. I call them glass-ceiling breakers because when they bought D-A-Y in 1969, women didn't own agencies of that size.

The first thing they did was create salary parity among the senior executives. When they got access to the books, they learned that many of the men who reported to them made substantially more than they did. But that's not what this story is about.

They must have seen something in me that I didn't see in myself, because they gave me countless opportunities to accelerate my agency career. Very early in my run, Jean called to say that we had the opportunity to pitch a record album, *Songs of the Great Depression.* (Even though the country had experienced a nostalgia wave recently, believe me, no one in 1980 wanted to hear this music!) And she wanted me to write the proposal.

Great news, right? Except I had never written a proposal, didn't know what to model it on, and wasn't smart enough to know what I didn't know or what to ask. I plunged in, and after a few days of staring at a blank word processor screen, I took it upon myself to call the president of the record label to ask for a few more days. (I wish I had the cojones now that I apparently had then!)

Within an hour or so, Jean asked me to come see her. Clueless to what it was about, I happily went to her office.

"So how's the proposal coming?" she asked, cool as a cucumber. "Well, Jean, it's a little tough. I'm stuck. So I called the president of the record label to ask for a few more days." "Yes, I know, he just phoned me."

Let's be honest, at that moment, she could have fired me for going over her head. She could have screamed at me. She could have, in the slang of the day "torn me a new one." And she wouldn't have been out of line to do any of those things. Instead she looked at me, rather kindly, and said, "Hmm. I wonder what other options you might have had." Immediately, the light bulb went off in my head.

"Oh, my God, Jean, I'm so sorry," I sputtered, as I shared all the choices I should have made rather than call the prospect. She looked at me, quite kindly, and said "Everyone can make mistakes here. The key is making them only once."

In that moment, if she had asked me to jump off a cliff, I truly would have gladly done so. A great leader, Jean chose empathy and kindness over anger, and used a question to get me thinking rather than telling me what I'd done wrong. In doing so, she created an intense moment of loyalty to her, that has lasted until today. (Jean passed away in 2011 at the age of 90.)

In full candor, during my agency years (1979 to 2006) I wasn't as effective a leader as Jean. I didn't always have her leadership wisdom, her kindness, and empathy towards all my team members.

But as a leadership coach (www.jacobscomm.com), I get to encourage my clients, who are mostly in PR and communications, to embrace Jean's legacy.

KEN JACOBS

PCC, CPC, ELI-MP, PRINCIPAL, JACOBS CONSULTING & EXECUTIVE COACHING

27

GIVEN—A SINGLE WORD IS ALL IT TAKES TO STAGE OUR TEAMS FOR SUCCESS

When obstacles appear and crises arise, it's a temptation to let circumstances become the reason that we can't create the results to which we have committed.

"Given" is a word that has become a favorite of mine to initiate a pivot to enable success. I have come to cherish this word because it can quickly get me and my team unstuck when faced with disruptions to my nicely laid out plans. It allows me to adjust to unexpected setbacks from a difficult or complicated reality. When reality dishes out challenges that initially look like brick walls, "given" reminds me that my circumstances don't have to determine my behavior. I can still achieve my goals by choosing the best action in the reality in which I find myself. When I find myself mired in the constraints that a difficult reality presents, I use "given" to help me to step into the power I have. It's a doorway to the space in which I can have impact.

"Given" begins a statement, which leads to a good question, which shows me I have choices to move forward: "Given that others are panicked by the loss of work, how can I remain calm and grounded?" "Given that this development has radically changed the demand for our current offerings, how can we adapt and create offerings that are relevant to today and valuable enough to restore revenue?"

Living in the mess at work and at home means we'll often confront what I call an "unpreferred" reality. When faced with an unpreferred reality, we overfocus on what we wish was different about the current state. We plow energy into defining, imagining, and fantasizing about how we would like things to be easier and less disruptive. But seriously, what power do we have to change the right now? While we rail against reality with fruitless arguments, reality folds its arms, leans back, and says, "This is what is. Period." You will lose any and all arguments with reality, but only 100% of the time.

The arguments will not only exhaust you; they'll also blind you to the power you have to co-create a different, more desired future. Arguing with reality robs you of the opportunity to be your best self in the moment. And just hoping things will get better can't affect the future. But there is a small space between an unpreferred reality and a preferred future where we can build a bridge. Actions in response to the moment can help co-create the future.

Your power resides in radically accepting what is, stopping the arguments, and resisting the urge to succumb to reality as if it were the only determinant of your future. "Given" greets reality with neutrality, free of story, and provides an antidote to suffering. It transmutes the details of reality's exceptional, powerful obstacles to a neutral view of how it is and what is possible in the midst of it. The word "given" locates the space in which to maneuver the escape hatch.

We often want to dream and scheme and think big, but sometimes, constructing a smaller, compact container for what can actually be done now can get us unstuck. "Given" shifts the energy away from the barriers of "why we can't" to the innovations of "how we could." It puts a focus on hope and gives us a role in its comeback.

The fastest way to alter an unpreferred reality is to stop the argument with that reality and put energy into co-creating a different future. Stop letting reality manufacture excuses for staying stuck, and recognize you are simply facing the circumstances in which you must act.

"Now" is what happens right before the future, and you have the power to connect the two. Given that life is always messy, "given" can keep you focused on what you can do or be in the moment to live happily.

CY WAKEMAN

PRESIDENT & FOUNDER, REALITY-BASED LEADERSHIP

ENABLING EMPLOYEES TO MEET THE MOMENT:

A GUIDE FOR SENIOR LEADERSHIP TEAMS

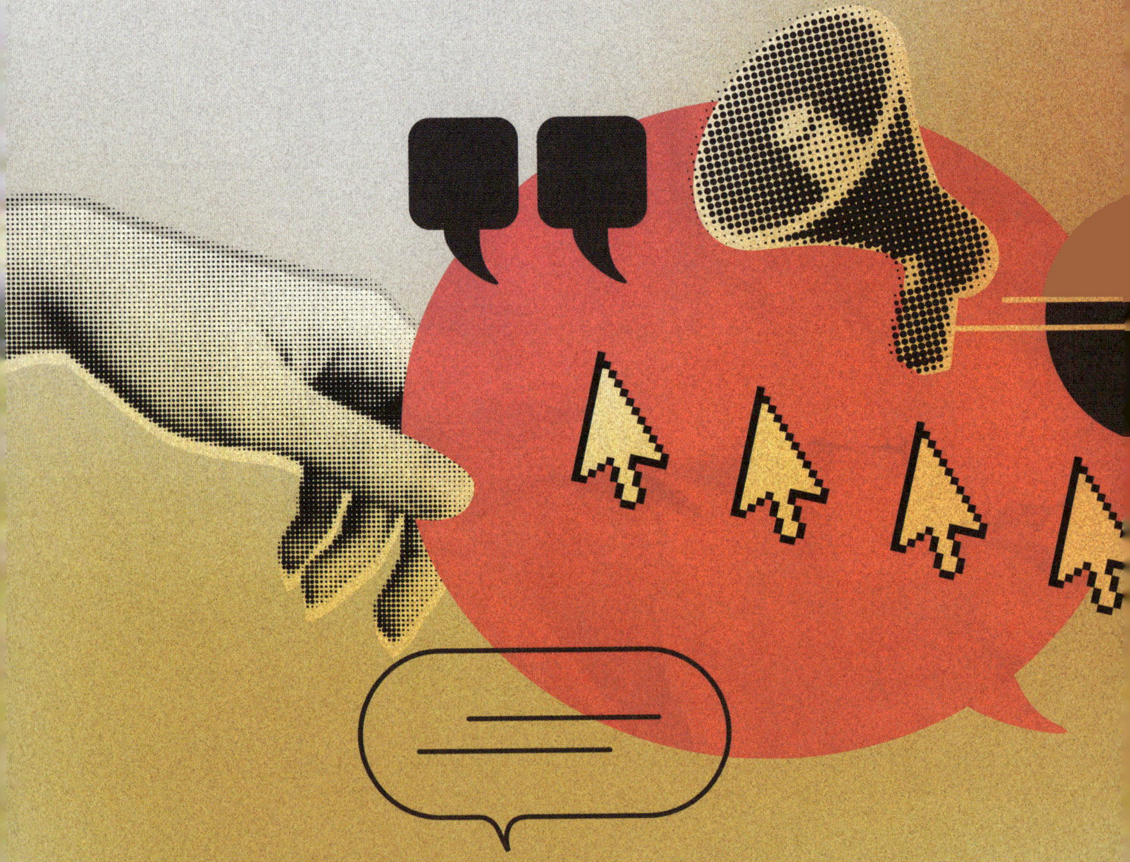

As a senior leadership team, your collective approach to enabling employees creates a multiplier effect that transforms both culture and results. When employees feel genuinely enabled to meet today's challenges, engagement soars, innovation accelerates, and your organization builds remarkable resilience. Here are the key actions your leadership team can take to make employee enablement your competitive advantage:

1 Establish a Strategic Talent-to-Work Alignment

Why This Matters: Senior teams that deeply understand the work that needs to be done and strategically match it with the right talent see significantly higher levels of performance and engagement.

Leadership Team Actions:

- Create an organizational skills inventory that maps to future needs
- Implement regular talent mapping against strategic priorities
- Develop cross-functional staffing approaches for key initiatives
- Build redeployment pathways to maximize existing talent
- Design succession planning with future capabilities in mind
- Create transparent career pathway opportunities across the organization

2 Build Systematic Collaboration Into Your Culture

Why This Matters: When collaboration becomes systematic rather than personality-dependent, innovation and problem-solving accelerate dramatically.

Leadership Team Actions:

- Remove department barriers
- Establish shared goals across silos
- Reward cross-team achievements
- Design physical and digital spaces that encourage connection
- Model collaborative leadership at the executive level

3 Expand Perspective Through External Connections

Why This Matters: Organizations that actively connect employees to outside perspectives avoid insularity and accelerate both growth and innovation.

Leadership Team Actions:

- Create industry exchange programs with partner organizations
- Establish customer immersion experiences for all employees
- Build communities of practice that extend beyond your organization
- Invite external perspectives to discussions
- Create a learning culture that values diverse perspectives

ENABLING EMPLOYEES TO MEET THE MOMENT:

A GUIDE FOR SENIOR LEADERSHIP TEAMS

4 Connect Individual Work to Organizational Purpose

Why This Matters:
Employees who clearly understand how their work contributes to organizational purpose bring significantly more discretionary effort and creativity to their roles.

Leadership Team Actions:

- Create clear line-of-sight from individual roles to strategic objectives
- Share impact stories that connect daily work to customer outcomes
- Develop purpose maps for teams and departments
- Build organizational purpose into recognition programs
- Include purpose alignment in performance discussions
- Regularly reinforce how each function contributes to the bigger picture

5 Deploy Technology with Intention and Humanity

Why This Matters:
Organizations that thoughtfully implement technology with a focus on employee experience create both productivity gains and cultural strength.

Leadership Team Actions:

- Evaluate all technology through an employee experience lens
- Create cross-functional technology selection teams
- Implement technology pilots before full deployment
- Provide adequate training and transition time for new systems
- Regularly audit technology stack for redundancy and effectiveness
- Establish clear metrics for technology's impact on both results and culture

6 Create an Environment of Psychological Safety

Why This Matters:
Teams that operate with high psychological safety innovate more effectively, surface problems earlier, and demonstrate greater resilience during change.

Leadership Team Actions:

- Model vulnerability and transparency in leadership communications
- Create formal mechanisms for surfacing and addressing concerns
- Reward productive dissent and constructive feedback
- Establish clear consequence-free channels for raising issues
- Measure psychological safety regularly through surveys and discussions
- Demonstrate how employee input shapes organizational decisions

QUESTIONS FOR YOUR NEXT SENIOR TEAM MEETING

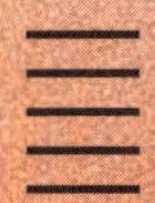

1. How effectively are we matching our talent to our highest-priority work?
2. Where do structural or cultural barriers prevent effective collaboration?
3. How are we deliberately bringing outside perspectives into our organization?
4. How well do our employees understand the connection between their work and our organizational purpose?
5. What's one immediate action we could take to better enable our employees to meet this moment?

REMEMBER:

The organizations that thrive in periods of rapid change are those where leadership teams make employee enablement a deliberate, strategic priority. By focusing on the right talent-work alignment, building systematic collaboration, expanding perspective, connecting work to purpose, deploying technology thoughtfully, and creating psychological safety, you establish the foundation for sustainable success in an ever-changing business landscape.

ACCESS POPULAR MEET THE MOMENT RESOURCES

FREE

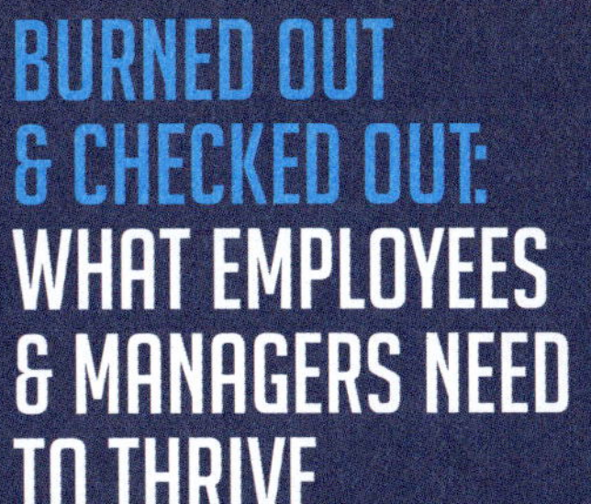

BURNED OUT & CHECKED OUT: WHAT EMPLOYEES & MANAGERS NEED TO THRIVE

Study

A PERSONA OF TODAY'S EMPLOYEE

eBook

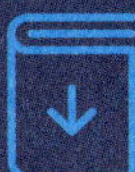

HOW TO BUILD TRUST IN THE WORKPLACE: THE ULTIMATE GUIDE FOR TODAY

Blog

> "The secret of getting ahead is getting started.
>
> - MARK TWAIN

MOVING FROM GOOD TO EXCEPTIONAL IN MODERN LEADERSHIP

Leadership isn't about perfection—it's about continuous growth, intentional practice, and a commitment to bringing out the best in yourself and those you lead. Our research also identified seven fundamental elements that transform how we connect, inspire, and drive organizational success.

These seven elements aren't checkboxes to complete—they're principles to internalize and practices to embed into the very fabric of your leadership approach.

Let's explore how you can elevate your leadership from good to exceptional...

GRATITUDE

The Transformative Power of Genuine Appreciation

Exceptional leaders understand that gratitude isn't a nice-to-have—it's a strategic imperative. It's about seeing and acknowledging the unique contributions that often go unnoticed. Appreciation isn't just saying "thank you"; it's creating moments that help people understand their true value and impact.

The power of gratitude extends far beyond momentary recognition. When leaders consistently and specifically appreciate their team's efforts, they create a ripple effect of motivation, engagement, and commitment. It transforms workplace dynamics from transactional interactions to meaningful connections where employees feel genuinely seen and valued. This isn't about empty praise, but about creating a culture of authentic recognition that aligns individual contributions with organizational success.

REFLECTION EXERCISE:

- Identify one team member whose consistent contributions you've overlooked
- Write a specific note detailing exactly what they do that makes a difference
- Share how their work connects to the broader organizational goals

CULTURE

Building an Environment Where People Thrive

Your culture is the invisible force that either propels your organization forward or holds it back. Exceptional leaders create "moments of belonging" where every team member knows they're part of something bigger than themselves. It's not about mission statements on walls—it's about how you show up every single day.

Culture isn't a static concept but a living, breathing ecosystem that requires constant nurturing. The most exceptional leaders understand that culture is built in small, consistent moments—how teams respond to challenges, support each other, and celebrate collective achievements. It's about creating an environment where innovation flourishes, where people feel psychologically safe to share ideas, and where the organization's values are not simply spoken, but lived authentically by every team member.

QUICK CULTURE ASSESSMENT:

- How do team members respond when:
    - Someone is struggling
    - A mistake is made
    - A new idea is presented
- What do these responses reveal about your current culture?

FIT

Connecting Individual Potential to Organizational Strategy

The most engaged employees aren't doing a job—they understand how their growth aligns with the organization's future. Exceptional leaders help team members see their unique place in the company's long-term talent strategy, transforming uncertainty into excitement and commitment.

Beyond simply matching skills to roles, true organizational fit is about creating a dynamic pathway of growth that benefits both the individual and the organization. It requires deep, ongoing conversations that go beyond annual performance reviews. Exceptional leaders become architects of potential, helping team members understand not only their current role, but the broader landscape of opportunities, skills they need to develop, and how their personal aspirations intersect with the organization's strategic direction.

PERSONAL DEVELOPMENT PROMPT:

- Map out potential career paths for key team members
- Identify the skills they need to develop
- Schedule conversations to discuss their aspirations and organizational opportunities

LISTENING

The Foundational Skill of Exceptional Leadership

True listening goes beyond hearing words—it's about creating a space of genuine understanding. Exceptional leaders don't solely wait to speak; they approach every conversation with radical curiosity, seeking to understand the human experience behind the words.

Listening is a complex skill that requires ongoing practice and intentionality. It's not about being quiet or allowing others to speak, but about creating psychological safety where people feel genuinely heard. The most exceptional leaders understand that listening is a strategic tool—it uncovers hidden insights, builds trust, and creates an environment where diverse perspectives can flourish. By listening, leaders transform communication from a one-way transmission to a collaborative dialogue that drives innovation and collective understanding.

LISTENING CHALLENGE:

- In your next three meetings, follow the 80/20 rule (listen 80% of the time, speak 20%)
- Ask clarifying questions
- Reflect back what you've heard before responding

EMPATHY

Creating Psychological Safety

Empathy isn't about agreeing with everything—it's about creating an environment where people feel genuinely seen and understood. Exceptional leaders recognize that empathy is a strategic skill that builds trust, drives innovation, and accelerates performance.

The most powerful form of empathy goes beyond emotional understanding—it's about creating tangible support that demonstrates genuine care. Exceptional leaders use empathy as a strategic tool, recognizing that when people feel understood, they become more resilient, more innovative, and more committed to collective success. This means creating systems and practices that show empathy isn't an individual skill, but an organizational commitment to supporting the whole person—their challenges, aspirations, and potential.

EMPATHY PRACTICE:

- Choose one team member facing a challenge
- Use the validation framework:
    - Acknowledge their experience
    - Ask what support looks like for them
    - Follow up with specific assistance

ACCOUNTABILITY

Leading by Example

Exceptional leaders hold themselves to the highest standards. Accountability isn't about punishment—it's about creating a culture of transparency, learning, and continuous improvement. When leaders model accountability, it becomes the norm, not the exception.

True accountability is a transformative leadership practice that goes beyond individual actions. It's about creating a culture where taking responsibility is seen as a strength, not a weakness. Exceptional leaders demonstrate this by openly sharing their own learning experiences, showing vulnerability, and creating systems that encourage honest reflection and growth. They understand that accountability is not about perfection, but about commitment to continuous improvement, learning from mistakes, and supporting team members in their own growth journeys.

ACCOUNTABILITY REFLECTION:

- Share a recent mistake with your team
- Explain what you learned
- Outline the steps you're taking to improve
- Invite feedback and input

WELL-BEING

Championing Holistic Success

Well-being is more than wellness programs—it's a comprehensive approach to supporting human potential. Exceptional leaders understand that peak performance comes from supporting the whole person, not the worker.

Holistic well-being requires a fundamental reimagining of how organizations support their people. It's not about isolated initiatives, but about creating an integrated approach that recognizes the interconnection between professional growth, mental health, personal development, and organizational success. Exceptional leaders view well-being as a strategic imperative—understanding that when people are supported in all dimensions of their lives, they bring their most innovative, committed, and authentic selves to work.

WELL-BEING AUDIT:

- Review your current support systems
- Identify gaps between organizational rhetoric and actual support
- Create a holistic well-being strategy that addresses:
    - Mental health
    - Professional development
    - Work-life integration
    - Personal growth opportunities

YOUR EXCEPTIONAL LEADERSHIP JOURNEY

REMEMBER:

Moving from good to exceptional isn't about achieving perfection. It's about consistent, intentional practice. Choose one element to focus on this quarter. Not all seven—just one. Dive deep. Make it a habit. Then, move to the next.

Leadership is a journey of continuous learning. The most exceptional leaders are those who remain curious, humble, and committed to growth—not solely for their organizations, but for themselves.

What will your first step be?

MODERN LEADERSHIP RESOURCE CENTER

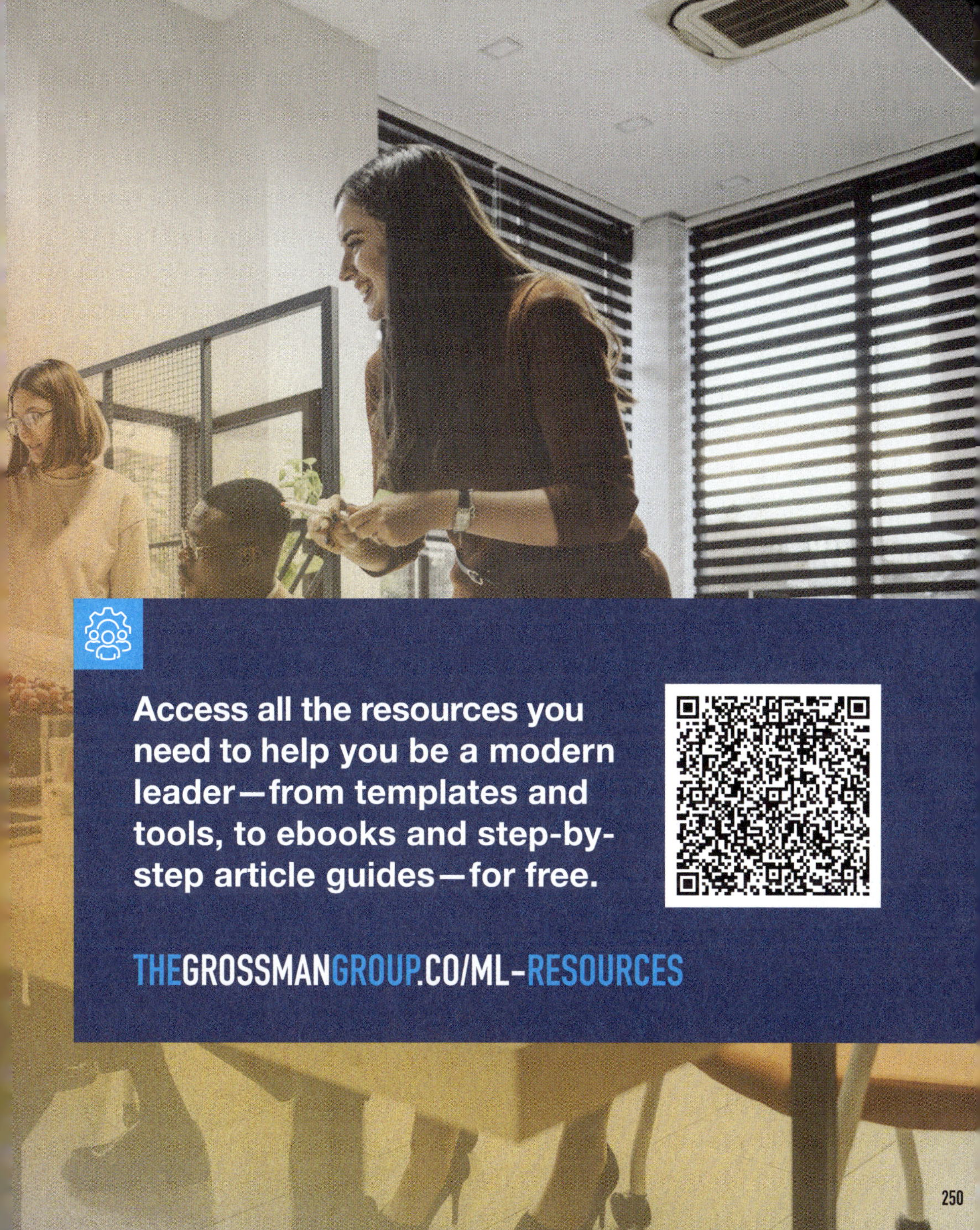
Access all the resources you need to help you be a modern leader—from templates and tools, to ebooks and step-by-step article guides—for free.
THEGROSSMANGROUP.CO/ML-RESOURCES

DAVID GROSSMAN

DAVID HELPS LEADERS MEET TODAY'S PRESSURES—AND RISE.

David Grossman is both a teacher and a student of leadership and communication. No surprise, he is one of America's foremost authorities—and a sought-after advisor to Fortune 500 companies. By acting as an advocate for employees and a **thought**partner™ to executives, David helps organizations meet the fast-evolving needs of today's workforce and soar.

David is founder and CEO of The Grossman Group, an award-winning Chicago-based agency focused on organizational consulting, strategic leadership, and internal communications. Clients include Abbott, Amsted, DHL, General Mills, Grubhub, Kimberly-Clark, Lockheed Martin, Novartis, and Stanley Black & Decker, among others.

A media source for his expert commentary and analysis on employee and leadership issues, David has been featured on "NBC Nightly News," *CBS MoneyWatch*, the *Chicago Tribune, Directors & Boards, Forbes, LA Times, Newsweek,* and the World Economic Forum.

David is a six-time author known most recently for his popular and award-winning Heart First series. ***Heart First:*** *What Exceptional Leaders Do in Extraordinary Times* is in its second edition and continues to be applauded for its practical approaches and rich stories of Heart First Leadership by executives around the globe.

David's leader**communicator**™ blog has been ranked the number-one blog on communications by Feedspot nine years in a row.

David is a member of the Forbes Communication Council, Page, the Public Relations Society of America (PRSA), the International Association of Business Communicators (IABC), and is a trustee to the board of the Institute for Public Relations (IPR).

The Grossman Group—a certified diversity supplier—has won all the "Oscars" of communication. The agency has been named PR Week's "Boutique Agency of the Year" (twice), as well as PRovoke Media's "Employee Communication Agency of the Year," PRSA's "Small Agency of the Year," and Ragan's "Agency of the Year." Prior to founding The Grossman Group in 2000, David was director of communications for McDonald's.

Connect with David today at David@TheGrossmanGroup.co.

BRING DAVID GROSSMAN TO YOUR STAGE

Turbulent times call for exceptional leadership. Are you ready?

David Grossman—award-winning speaker, communication strategist, and coach to the C-Suite—delivers the groundbreaking keynotes leaders need to navigate today's complexities.

In his latest offering, David draws on his research with The Harris Poll and reveals that only 30% of leaders meet the fast-evolving needs of today's workforce.

You face mounting pressures—from shareholder value to AI, geopolitical swings, and more.

The good news is, it's not an impossible job...if you have the adaptive mindset required for fast-changing environments. David cites that exceptional leaders integrate emotional intelligence with strategic thinking. He calls this "leading with their heart IN their head."

In practice, that looks like compassion with calculation. Empathy with analysis. Values with decisions. The impact is greater, more sustainable performance for you, your team, and your organization.

Your rise from good to great can start now.

Check David's schedule today at David@TheGrossmanGroup.co.

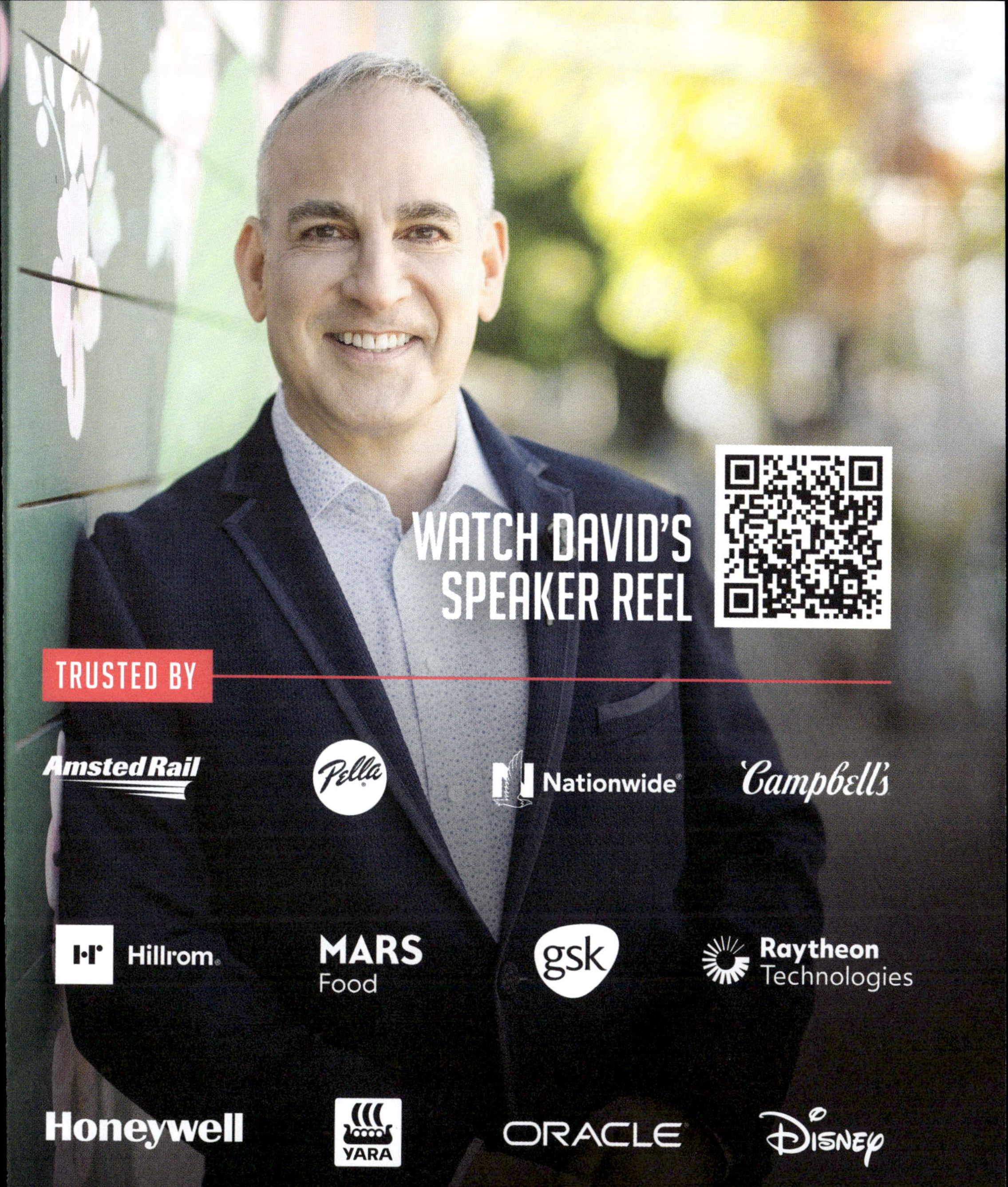
WATCH DAVID'S SPEAKER REEL
TRUSTED BY
AmstedRail
Pella
Nationwide
Campbell's
Hillrom
MARS Food
gsk
Raytheon Technologies
Honeywell
YARA
ORACLE
Disney

YOUR PARTNER IN CHANGE:

ALIGNING STRATEGY, CULTURE, COMMUNICATION & TEAMS

The Grossman Group is an award-winning communications consulting firm helping senior leaders and their teams:

- Activate strategy with leader alignment and communication that accelerates results
- Lead through change with clarity, confidence, and alignment
- Transform culture to improve engagement and performance
- Elevate internal communication to world-class standards
- Inspire and equip employees to drive business success

Your Partner in Success

We don't just advise—we roll up our sleeves and work alongside you. As seamless extensions of your team, we help you deliver meaningful results while making your job easier. And while we take our work seriously, we believe collaboration should be enjoyable, too.

CALL US: 312.829.3252

EMAIL US: David@TheGrossmanGroup.co

LEARN MORE: TheGrossmanGroup.co

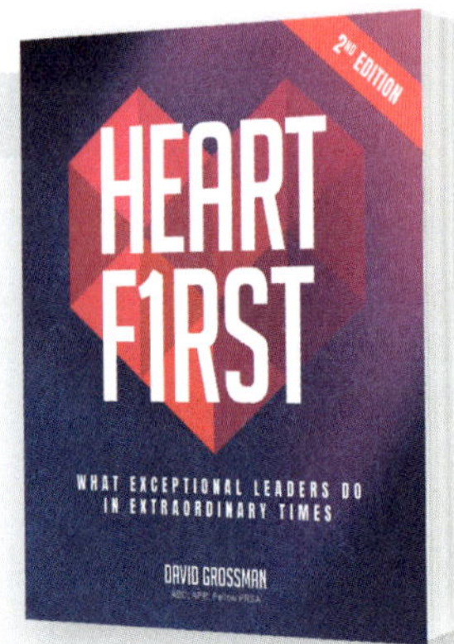

Inspired and inspiring—that is what Heart First is for leaders.

- Farah Speer, SVP, Corporate Communications and External Relations, AviadoBio

David does a beautiful job capturing real-life lessons learned from the front lines of pandemic and social change related communications.

- Cy Wakeman, New York Times bestselling author of No Ego

Heart First is loaded with powerful stories and valuable tips for all leaders and those aspiring to become authentic leaders.

- Ron Culp, Professional Director, Public Relations & Advertising Program, DePaul University

"

Practical, wise, smartly designed—an example of what it recommends to its readers.

- Jon Iwata, Senior Vice President, Marketing and Communications, IBM Corporation

"

A must-read highlighting the importance of communication in bridging the organization's strategies and goals with an individual's performance.

- Norm Wesley, Former Chairman and CEO, Fortune Brands

"

Strong communication is the lifeblood of effective execution, and David cuts to the chase with insightful roadmaps for leaders.

- Teresa Paulsen, Vice President, Communication & External Relations, ConAgra Foods

RESEARCH METHODOLOGY

The survey was conducted online within the United States between June 18th-21st and July 9th-11th 2024, among 2,206 employed adults (aged 18 and over) by The Harris Poll on behalf of The Grossman Group.

Data were weighted where necessary by age, gender, race/ethnicity, region, education, marital status, household size, household income, and political party affiliation, to bring them in line with their actual proportions in the population.

Respondents for this survey were selected from among those who have agreed to participate in our surveys. The sampling precision of Harris online polls is measured by using a Bayesian credible interval. For this study, the sample data is accurate to within + 2.5 percentage points using a 95% confidence level. This credible interval will be wider among subsets of the surveyed population of interest.

All sample surveys and polls, whether or not they use probability sampling, are subject to other multiple sources of error which are most often not possible to quantify or estimate, including but not limited to coverage error, error associated with nonresponse, error associated with question wording and response options, and post-survey weighting and adjustments.

The research first appears on page xxxi.

FRAMEWORK METHODOLOGY

The Seven Elements on the Path from Good to Exceptional in Modern Leadership.

In this study, we employed Partial Least Squares Structural Equation Models (PLS-SEM) to explore the factors that drive employees' perceptions of "exceptional leadership" within their company. This technique allows us to group measured variables into themed latent constructs before modeling their relationship to the dependent variable[1]. This approach was selected with the idea of simplifying the analysis and dealing with high multi-collinearity among many of the measured survey attributes. A principal component analysis (PCA) was conducted on the survey data to first identify latent variables to use in the PLS-SEM model. The constructs in this model were represented as "reflective" constructs, meaning that the survey attributes were assumed to be manifestations of the construct that they were assigned.

To better understand the impact of these latent constructs on exceptional leadership, we conducted a Johnson's Relative Importance Analysis[2]. This analysis allowed us to measure the relative importance, as a percent (%) estimate, of each latent construct with respect to exceptional leadership. Additionally, the relative importance of the attributes within each construct was measured by the proportion of summed loadings.

The framework first appears on page xxxix.

REFERENCES

[1]Hair, J., Hult, G. T. M., Ringle, C. M., & Sarstedt, M. (2016). A primer on partial least squares structural equation modeling (PLS-SEM) (2nd ed.). SAGE Publications.

[2]Johnson, J. W. (2000). A heuristic method for estimating the relative weight of predictor variables in multiple regression. Multivariate Behavioral Research, 35, 1-19.